IMAGES
of America

DELTAVILLE

The schooner *Maggie* was built in 1871 in Dorchester County, Maryland. Jackson Creek was the home port for the schooner in the 1930s and 1940s when it was owned by Capt. Tom Henry Ruark of Deltaville. Here, the boat is anchored in Fishing Bay, showing its bow rigging in 1946 at Deagle and Son Marine Railway. (Courtesy of Dr. A.L. VanName Jr.)

ON THE COVER: The Deltaville community held annual Fourth of July boat races on Fishing Bay for many years. This photograph was taken around 1948, when Jimmy Pretty of Richmond outdistanced all challengers in his homemade race boat as spectators watched from yachts, skiffs, and traditional wooden workboats, all pictured. (Courtesy of Carolyn Norton Schmalenberger and Billy Norton.)

IMAGES
of America

DELTAVILLE

Larry S. Chowning

ARCADIA
PUBLISHING

Published by Arcadia Publishing
Charleston, South Carolina

Library of Congress Control Number: 2013949593

For all general information, please contact Arcadia Publishing:
Telephone 843-853-2070
Fax 843-853-0044
E-mail sales@arcadiapublishing.com
For customer service and orders:
Toll-Free 1-888-313-2665

Visit us on the Internet at www.arcadiapublishing.com

Dedicated to the memory of Hugh and Dorothy Norris,
Willis and Elizabeth Wilson, Lewis Wright, Wilbur Denvy
"Dink" Miller, Molly "Crab" Weston, Talmadge and Edmond
Ruark, Grover Lee Owens, and Capt. Johnny Ward.

CONTENTS

ACKNOWLEDGMENTS

I want to thank all those who have assisted me in this effort to produce a photographic history of the community of Deltaville. Without your help, this would not have been possible. Those who contributed include Willard and Shirley Norris, Norton Hurd, Garland Robins, Betsy Hudgins, Carolyn Norton Schmalenberger, Alfred E. Ailsworth Jr., Gene Ruark, Ed Deagle, Fred and Jane Crittenden, Billy Norton, Walter Allen and Betty Harrow, Norman Hall, Charles A. "Duck" Ruark, Dr. Edwin Ruark, Tyler Crittenden, James "Turk" Crittenden, Vera and John England, Emily Chowning, Selden Richardson, Fred and Bettie Lee Gaskins, Julie Burwood, Joe Gaskins, Tom Hardin, the *Southside Sentinel*, William C. Hight, John and Susan Collamore, Middlesex County Public Library, Raynell Smith, Deltaville Maritime Museum, Holly Horton, Helen Chandler, Marilyn South, Middlesex County Museum, John M. Bareford Jr., Betty Chowning, Diane Batley Dalsaso, Pete Letcher, Lynne Phillips, Chesapeake Bay Maritime Museum, Lynn Dunlevy, Middlesex County Clerk's Office, Joe Conboy, Beverly and Jamie Barnhardt, Harvey and Clemmie Langford, Billy and Mabel Williams, Claudia Soucek, Frances Hall, Bob Strotmeyer, Pam Strotmeyer, George and Frauline Robinson, First Baptist of Amburg, Jere and Paula Dennison, Edmond Harrow Jr., Donovan Masonic Lodge, Edna Shackelford, Judy Richwine, Randolph Norton, Thomas R. "Dickie" Marshall, Dick Murray, Caroline Jones, Deborah Haynes, Jimmy Johnson, Carolyn Henkel, Paris Ashton, Graham Jones Jr., Robert Cerullo, Alfred Scott, Strother Scott, Juanita Glascock, and Bob Lackey.

INTRODUCTION

On July 17, 1608, the year after Jamestown was settled, Capt. John Smith and 14 men explored the Chesapeake Bay. Just off a point of land in shallow water, they began spearing fish with their swords for sustenance. Smith stabbed a fish and pulled it to the surface. The fish turned out to be a stingray, and as it surfaced, its poisonous tail punctured Smith's arm. His health quickly deteriorated. Fearing he would die, his colleagues began to dig him a proper grave—but he survived. He later jokingly remarked that once he felt better he ate the ray for supper. In 1612, when Smith published the first complete map of Chesapeake Bay, he named this point of land "Stingray Isle." Today, it is known as Stingray Point, Deltaville, Virginia.

During America's colonial period, the farming of tobacco was the main source of livelihood in the area. The rich, sandy soil found along creeks and rivers of Virginia was extremely advantageous to growing a lucrative "sweet-scented" tobacco. That tobacco became extremely popular in England; during the 1620s, the rising price of tobacco brought hundreds of new colonists into Virginia as they sought their fortunes.

By 1640, there were 8,000 settlers in Virginia and not enough unsecured acreage along the James and York Rivers to accommodate either the number of tobacco-growers wanting to expand their business or the new ones wanting to get into the trade. In 1642, the first English land grants were issued on the Piankatank River. There were eight all together, and the first grant in Middlesex County was Barn Elms, located near Hartfield and just down the road from Deltaville. Col. John Matrum received that grant for 1,900 acres on July 20, 1642; the land was named Matrum's Mount.

On August 10 of the same year, Thomas Trotter and Peregine Bland received grants of 500 and 1,000 acres respectively on the Piankatank that included some land that is today part of Deltaville. In 1644, a major Native American uprising occurred, resulting in nearly 500 English being killed. Royal governor William Berkeley called all English families living in the recently settled territories to move back to the York River. The Deltaville plantation settlements were abandoned and in 1646, a treaty between the English and Indians gave that land on the Piankatank back to the Native Americans.

By 1649, Virginia had grown to 15,000 English settlers and new treaties opened up areas around the Piankatank and Rappahannock Rivers for permanent settlement. English control of the land along those rivers and Chesapeake Bay was now finalized. One of the first written mentions of a location in the Deltaville area came in February 1653, when Englishman Thomas Bourn received a land grant that stated "with a western branch of Piankatank opposite to Store Point." Today, that area of the community is called Stove Point. The last recorded record that used Store Point was John Berry's will dated December 9, 1766, that states, "I give my son John Berry II all that parcel of land I bought of Philip Grymes, Esq. commonly known by the name of Store Point." By the hand of a careless scribe, Store Point became Stove Point ever after.

With Deltaville's location wedged between two major rivers and its easternmost shores touching the Chesapeake Bay, much of America's colonial, antebellum, and Civil War history unfolded right before the eyes of those living in the region.

The Fry-Jefferson Map of Virginia, dated 1751, notes Stingray Point, Store Point, Churchill, and Kemps as locations in and around what is today Deltaville. The Churchill family owned large acreage that reached from the Rappahannock to the Piankatank, in areas called Bushy, Wake, Hartfield, and Wilton. The Kemp family owned acreage between Hartfield and Stove Point on the Piankatank, which included some Deltaville land. Kemp's (tobacco) warehouse and gristmill served people in that region. The warehouse was destroyed when accidentally set afire in 1776 by a company of American minutemen stationed there.

Lights of the Revolutionary War were most visible to the people in the Deltaville area in September 1781, when a fleet of vessels anchored just inside the mouth of the Piankatank River. British plundering of homes and property along the Deltaville shoreline caused concern. The lights, however, were not from British ships, but from American vessels. The fleet was loaded with flour and food bound for Gloucester County to assist in feeding the American army involved in battle with the English at Yorktown, the battle that ended the American Revolution.

Deltaville men fought in every war and on both sides in the Civil War, Union and Confederate. All the wars fought on United States soil directly impacted the local populace. Providence on the Piankatank was raided by Lord Dunmore's troops in the Revolution, and two Confederate soldiers who took refuge there were killed when they were found and dragged from one of the upstairs rooms. Union soldiers shot them at the front gate, leaving the bodies to be buried in the cemetery at Providence.

The War of 1812 was as challenging for Deltaville residents as the Revolutionary or Civil War. The area was under blockade for much of the war as British ships were regularly coming into the area. On April 3, 1813, Deltaville residents standing on the banks of the Rappahannock witnessed the Battle of the Rappahannock, where British sailors defeated an American warship fleet in a gun battle.

During the Civil War, the local populace regularly faced Union and Confederate activity. The 36th US Colored Infantry invaded Middlesex and fought a skirmish near Wake against a small group of Confederate troops and sympathizers. Three hundred black troops, some former slaves from the area, arrived on Deltaville shores on May 12, 1864. They burned a mill, captured Confederate torpedoes, and killed and captured Confederate sympathizers and soldiers home on leave. They camped at Fishing Bay.

On August 18, 1863, Union troops raided the residence of Thomas Hutchins, whose home was on the road leading to Providence and Lucy's Cove. Hutchins was accused by a slave named Warner of firing at Union gunboats from the shore. Unable to find him, they ransacked his home and shot his cows dead in the fields. Hutchins was a community leader and was on the first board of trustees of Clarksbury Methodist Church. About the same time, Confederate officer John Taylor Wood and Confederate president Jefferson Davis concocted a secret plan for a strike force to capture Yankee gunboats with so-called Horse Marines. Battle activities took place in and around Deltaville. Union ships were captured right off the shores of Stingray Point and the sounds of pistols firing and men dying could be heard through the open windows of homes in Deltaville.

Peaceful times were to come to the Deltaville community. Throughout its history, the rivers and bay provided livelihood and sustenance and were the lifeblood of the community. The wind and sea provided jobs for men aboard sailing schooners, steamboats, and freighters; and oysters, fish, and crabs were caught from the bay's waters and marketed by Deltaville watermen. But one of the most remarkable eras came in the early part of the 20th century and lasted through the 1990s, as Deltaville became the wooden-boatbuilding capital of Chesapeake Bay, where deadrise and cross-planked boats were built and sold far and wide. The Deltaville Deadrise became a name known all over Chesapeake Bay. Even more specifically, Jackson Creek Round Sterns and Broad Creek Round Sterns further delineated the location where the boats were built. When a Rock Hall, Maryland, waterman said with pride that he owned a Jackson Creek Round Stern, watermen from Cape Henry, Virginia, to Havre de Grace, Maryland, knew that it was Deltaville built. Broad and Jackson Creeks were center stage in the bay's boatbuilding industry. This would carry forth into the modern-day economic growth of the community.

As boats were being constructed in the backyards of Deltaville, people came to town to see their boats built and watch the progress. Later, when their boats needed repair and maintenance, they brought them back to have them worked on by the men who knew their boats best. Small marine railways were installed along the shores to haul the boats in and out of the water. Over time, the boatbuilding culture and infrastructure led to larger railways and the servicing of larger boats. This led to the rise of the modern-day marinas that today are the economic lifeblood of the community. During the summer months, Deltaville's population triples as folks from Richmond and elsewhere come to town to play on their boats, eat out at restaurants, buy fishing line at Hurd's, purchase fresh seafood from J.&W. Seafood, and enjoy the sweet summer air of Chesapeake Bay. As a tribute to the community's maritime heritage, the Deltaville Maritime Museum officially opened April 29, 2003, on the banks of Mill Creek, just a short distance from where old Jackson Creek Wharf once stood. In 1989, longtime resident of Deltaville Pette Clark gave Holly Point, 37 acres of waterfront property, to Middlesex County. Gene Ruark, a board member of the Deltaville Community Association, asked the county board of supervisors for support in using Holly Point as a site for the museum. The museum has become one of the most popular locations in Deltaville and is well known throughout the region.

Deltaville evolved from the many little post offices in the area. Since the community has never been an incorporated town with specific town boundaries, Deltaville grew out of several small communities. Stingray Point is the eastern most tip of Deltaville. Watermark dates for the Point were 1858, when Stingray Point Lighthouse was erected, and May 10, 1940, when Stingray Point was designated an official United States post office. The post office closed August 14, 1941, as part of the consolidation that eventually led to the single post office in the Deltaville area.

In 1898, the community of Ruark on Fishing Bay was designated a post office, which was closed in 1933. The largest Deadrise wooden-motorized boat built on Chesapeake Bay was constructed in 1927 at Price's Marine Railway in Ruark. The Marydel measured 97 feet, 7.2 inches by 28 feet, 2 inches by 7 feet, 7 inches and was used to haul fertilizer. In the 1930s, the community of Ruark was also the loading and off-loading spot for the Richmond-Eastern Shore Ferry across Chesapeake Bay from Harborton on the Eastern Shore of Virginia to Deltaville. The ferry held 40 cars and ran a three-hour crossing. In 1948, Urbanna Yacht Club purchased 2.41 acres of land on Stove Point and moved there, renaming the club Fishing Bay Yacht Club. A clubhouse was built and annual sailboat races were held.

The westernmost portion of Deltaville is Amburg. The community had a post office from 1891 to 1977. The mail then went to Deltaville Post Office. Enoch Post Office was at Jackson Creek Wharf, near the mouth of Mill and Jackson Creeks. It was founded in 1885 and discontinued in 1913. Grinels was a post office at North End Wharf started in 1885 and discontinued in 1908, when mail went to Amburg. Grinels Post Office reopened in 1911 and closed permanently April 30, 1934, nine months after the August Storm of 1933 destroyed the North End and Jackson Creek Wharfs. Another post office in the Deltaville area was Kram, founded in 1902 and closed to be part of Amburg in 1903. Conrad's Mill was an official post office from 1878, discontinued in 1905 to be part of Wilton Post Office. Between Conrad's Mill and Amburg is Hardyville, which was founded in 1922 and where the post office is still in operation.

Deltaville grew from all of these areas, but most prominently from Sandy Bottom. Founded August 20, 1835, it was the central post office in the area and one of the oldest in Middlesex County. The first postmaster was Lewis L. Stiff. The Vaughan and Crittenden families were most numerous as postmasters there. The only female postmaster of Sandy Bottom in its 74-year history was Julia W. Vaughan, who held the position in 1894.

Sandy Bottom Post Office officially closed December 3, 1909, the same day Deltaville Post Office opened. The last Sandy Bottom and the first Deltaville postmaster was Lester C. "Clyde"

Crittenden. He was the Deltaville postmaster for 32 years, until 1941, and had been in charge of the Sandy Bottom since 1906.

The area known as Deltaville was once called Unionville, named after Union Church, an interdenominational church located just east of Sandy Bottom Post Office. Since the new post office was going to be located near where the church had been, a petition was circulated to change the name to Unionville. Will Thomas recommended that the name be Delta, rather than Unionville, as the old church was no longer functioning and the land along the shores of the community formed a delta. There had also been a Delta Academy in the community in the 1890s and this may have contributed to the name. Virginia, however, already had a Delta Post Office and the request was denied by the postal system. The community then decided on Deltaville. The name stuck and the community has grown and prospered ever since.

The strength of this tight-knit community is most apparent during adversity. On April 16, 2011, a tornado struck the heart of Deltaville, causing $6.8 million in property damage. The twister demolished the stately Zoar Baptist Church and over 30 homes and structures. The Deltaville Community Association Building—formerly the cafeteria at Deltaville School built in the 1930s under the auspices of the Works Progress Administration—and the community swimming pool were damaged. The community rallied together, and in less than a year, the pool and community center were repaired, mostly with private funds and labor. In September 2013, Zoar Baptist Church held a dedication service in a new sanctuary.

On July 18, 2012, tragedy struck again when the Deltaville Maritime Museum's main building and outside boat pavilion were destroyed by fire. Once again, the community rallied behind the slogan "the things you do for yourself are gone when you are gone, but the things you do for others remain as your legacy." The museum was rebuilt and continues to educate people on the importance of the maritime heritage and culture of Deltaville, Virginia.

Today, Deltaville is a major boating community on the bay and lives up to its new name, recently endorsed by the Middlesex County Board of Supervisors, as the "Boating Capital of the Chesapeake."

One

EARLY DAYS

John Smith and his band of explorers in 1608 were perhaps the first Englishmen to set foot on Deltaville soil, but American Indians had been there for several thousand years before. The Piankatank and Rappahannock Rivers on the south and north sides of Deltaville are named for the two Indian tribes that lived along the shores. Store Point, the early name for Stove Point between Fishing Bay and Chesapeake Bay, is believed to have been an Indian and English trading post utilized by those passing by in boats. Deltaville's Bland Point is named after Peregrine Bland, who received a land grant of 1,000 acres in that area in August 1642, the first year of settlement.

The plantation system that grew out of the tobacco economy in Deltaville gave rise to several large plantations in the vicinity. Bushy Park, the ancestral estate of the Virginia branch of the Churchill family, was located in the Wake area, just west of Deltaville. The manor house at Bushy Park burned around 1760, and the family built Wilton in the 1770s on the Piankatank River.

Barn Elms, the home of the Berkeley family, was located on the Piankatank River near Hartfield. During the Revolutionary War, Edmund Berkeley IV was Middlesex County's representative at four Virginia Conventions and was a burgess for Middlesex from 1773 to 1776. He was a key person in bringing the Revolutionary War spirit to Deltaville and Middlesex County.

Berry Ville, situated on the Piankatank, is believed to have been built in 1750 and is still standing today. Providence, near Pace's Neck, was plundered during the Revolutionary War by British troops. Other pre–Revolutionary War plantations were Fairfield Plantation and Bath Farm at Hartfield, very near the Anglican chapel of Lower Church, which is still in service today as Lower United Methodist Church.

Barn Elms was located just west of Deltaville on the Piankatank River and was home to Col. Edmund Berkeley IV. He represented Middlesex County and Deltaville at four Virginia Conventions and was a burgess from 1773 to 1776. He was a key person in bringing the Revolutionary War spirit to the county and conveying that spirit to other Virginians. (Courtesy of Betty Chowning.)

During the Revolutionary War, the Colonial home of Wilton, not far from Deltaville on Piankatank River, was owned by Virginia militia officer Col. William Churchill, who was also clerk of Middlesex County court from 1772 to 1799. During a British raid of Wilton in 1781, the home was plundered and Churchill was dragged from his home and taken aboard a British warship. He was later released. (Courtesy of Betty Chowning.)

Providence is a pre–Revolutionary War home that was invaded by British sailors during the Revolution and by Union soldiers in the Civil War. A Union gunboat shelled Providence and a cannonball struck the kitchen wall. Owner William Vaughan's four sons were killed in the war and all buried in Providence's cemetery. Also buried there are two Confederate soldiers who Union troops killed after finding them hiding in an upstairs bedroom. (Courtesy of Betty Chowning.)

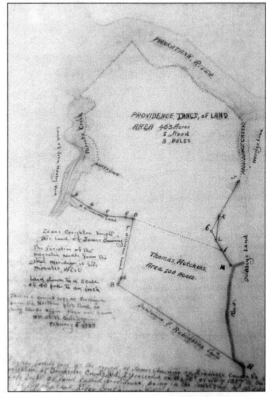

This 1820s survey shows Moore Creek was then named Parrots Creek, and Core Creek was Providence Creek. During the Civil War and before, Thomas Hutchens owned 100 acres of land near Lucy's Cove, as noted on the survey. On August 17, 1863, Union troops "desolated the home of Mr. Hutchins, carrying off everything possible and shooting his stock in the field," according to the *Richmond Daily Dispatch*. (Courtesy of Middlesex County Clerk's Office.)

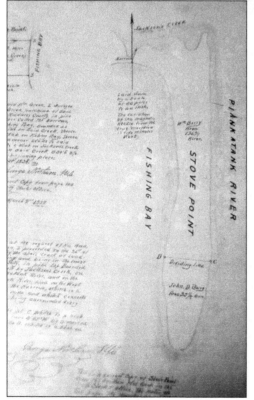

Sheep grazed on the lawn at Woodport in the early part of the 20th century. When Washington's army was fighting at Yorktown during the Revolutionary War, Deltaville and other surrounding areas were required to supply "beef and mutton" to help feed the American force. The Army required that 10 percent of the animals owned by each family be provided to feed the troops. (Courtesy of Beverly and Jamie Barnhardt.)

William Berry and John D. Berry owned Stove Point in the 1820s. The Berry family bought it in 1761 for five shillings from Phillip Grymes. On the survey, the *v* in Stove could well be mistaken for a lowercase *r*. Originally, Stove Point was named Store Point, and legend has it that it was an Indian trading post. Thus it was named Store Point, but sometime in history, the *r* was changed to a *v*. (Courtesy of Middlesex County Clerk's Office.)

Located at the head of Wilton Creek, a few miles west of Deltaville, Conrad's Mill was a gristmill that served the Deltaville Community. White corn and wheat were ground into cornmeal and flour. Deltaville residents brought their grain to be milled and fished and swam in the millpond while waiting. On special occasions, Conrad's Mill Pond was used as a setting for baptismal services by area Baptists who practiced immersion. (Courtesy of Violene Jackson.)

OLD MILL IN MIDDLESEX CO. VA.

New Market was the home of the Jackson family, some of whom are pictured here. James H. Jackson is believed to have built New Market right after the Civil War. He ran a general merchandise store on the corner of the home lot. New Market was later owned by M.A. Jackson, who ran a store and post office named Enoch on Jackson Creek Steamboat Wharf. (Courtesy of Jerome Jackson.)

This early-1900s photograph is of William Henry Norton and family. The home is a typical style of clapboard house that was built on Lovers Lane in the 19th century. The style was called a shotgun house because a person can see through the front door and out to the backyard through the back door. There was also a dogtrot connecting the main house to the kitchen. (Courtesy of Randolph Norton.)

The Kelly House in the heart of Deltaville was the home of William Henry Kelly and his wife, Nancy. They moved from Baltimore to occupy the home in 1858. Although he lived in a Confederate state, Kelly enlisted in the Union army when war broke out. Union troops took Nancy's cow, but returned it when they learned that her husband was fighting on their side. (Author's collection.)

This photograph, taken in 1933, shows that Stove Point was at one time mostly trees and a field. On the isthmus between Ruark and Stove Point is a small pond. This area is called the Narrows and was used by Deltaville men to drag small boats from Jackson Creek across to Fishing Bay rather than make the journey around the end of Stove Point. Tobacco Cove, at the north end of Stove Point inside Jackson Creek, most likely got its name in the days when tobacco was the money crop of the region and English ships arrived to carry it across the Atlantic. (Courtesy of Middlesex County Museum.)

Two

SAILING DAYS
AND LIGHTHOUSES

The location of Deltaville near the Chesapeake Bay encouraged many Deltaville men to go to sea on sail-powered freighting vessels—schooners, rams, and pungies. The location also brought sailors to its shores.

James Norris was a sea captain from Hyannis Port, Massachusetts, who skippered an oceangoing sailing vessel. On a trip south in the early 1800s, he came inside the bay and moored off Jackson Creek. He came ashore and met a sweet little 15-year-old Virginia girl. They fell in love and got married. This started a long tradition of Norris family members living in Deltaville and working aboard sailboats.

Sometime in the late 1800s, Capt. Phil Ruark was sailing near Deltaville and, as so often happened in those days, he went ashore to do some courting. There, he met his wife-to-be, Ida Blanche Johnston. After he was married, he moved to Deltaville near Fishing Bay. His first cousin Al moved there too, which started a tradition of Ruarks in the freighting business.

At the turn of the 20th century, there were nearly 800 sailing freighting vessels in the bay waters hauling lumber, coal, pig iron, fertilizer, potatoes, oysters, watermelons, canned vegetables and fruit—whatever there was to haul. Deltaville families with names such as Norris, Ruark, Ward, Ailsworth, Taylor, Wright, Bratton, Norton, Games, Mason, and Johnston made their livings sailing the Chesapeake Bay. This tradition is alive today in the Ward family of Jackson Creek, which owns and operates several tugboats and barges used to haul grain and other freight, after a long tradition of owning and working oyster buy boats in the decades before.

The constant maritime activity in and around Deltaville prompted the United States Coast Guard to build Stingray Point Lighthouse in 1858 on the shoal between the Rappahannock and Piankatank Rivers. The hexagonal, screw-pile lighthouse was a fixture in the community until it was decommissioned and dismantled in 1965.

During the Civil War, the lighthouse was not only a navigational aid, but it was also used as an Underground Railroad station where Union ships picked up runaway slaves who had rowed or paddled their small crafts to freedom.

Lighthouse keepers were revered, and many in Deltaville still recall the names of Richard M. Glenn, James Thomas Parks, Julian Jarvis, Larry Marchant, and John T. Saunders as those who kept the lighthouse beacon lit.

The sailing schooner *Maggie* was built in 1871 in Dorchester, Maryland, and was abandoned at Rockland, Maine in 1955. For most of its life, it sailed on Chesapeake Bay. Tom Henry Ruark of Deltaville owned *Maggie* in the 1940s, and its home port was Jackson Creek. Many a Deltaville lad found employment on the boats that hauled oysters and bulk freight. (Courtesy of Dr. A.L. VanName Jr.)

This photograph was taken at Fishing Bay around 1946 when the sailing schooner *Maggie* was at anchor. The catboat seen here belonged to the Strotmeyers, a Richmond family who started coming to the Ruark area in the early 1930s. (Courtesy of Bob Strotmeyer.)

The *Columbia F.C.*, shown here, was owned by Edmond Ruark of Deltaville. It could hold 9,000 cases of tomato cans that were hauled from Baltimore to H.T. Daniels and Son Tomato Factory in Amburg, just west of Deltaville. Often, Ruark hauled a load of lumber from Deltaville to Baltimore and brought back tomato cans. (Courtesy of Dr. A.L. VanName Jr.)

This photograph, taken in the early 1940s, is of Capt. Tom Henry Ruark (right) and his son Capt. Edmond Ruark, who were the last two Deltaville sailors to own commercial sailing schooners. They are relaxing on Tom Henry's side porch after returning home from delivering a load of freight. Going back to the 1700s, the men of Deltaville have a long involvement in commercial sail. (Courtesy of Charles A. Ruark.)

The 80-foot *Annie M. Leonard* was built in 1877 as a sailing schooner. Still under sail, its name was changed in 1913 to the *Lula M. Phillips*. It was converted to a powerboat some years later and owned by Capt. Will Ward of Deltaville. The boat's home port was Jackson Creek. (Courtesy of Dr. A.L. VanName Jr.)

James H. Jackson and his son, Sam, owned a store on the edge of James's property, a home that is still standing today and named New Market. This invoice, dated September 3, 1877, from Jackson's New Market store, also mentions the schooner *Thomas J. Jackson*. The schooner was built the same year of the invoice in Middlesex County, where Deltaville is located. (Courtesy of Willard and Shirley Norris.)

The sailing schooner *Columbia F.C.* was built at Mundy Point, Virginia, in 1874, for the Columbia Fishing Club in Washington, DC, and its name was derived from that sporting organization. Its home port in the 1940s was Jackson Creek. (Courtesy of Dr. A.L. VanName Jr.)

This stern photograph of the *Columbia F.C.* was taken in 1946. Capt. Edmond Ruark was the last generation of Ruark family to make a living hauling freight aboard sailing vessels. Ruark hauled vegetable cans from Baltimore to tomato-canning factories, lumber to Baltimore, seed oysters from the James River, and fertilizer and coal from Norfolk. (Courtesy of Dr. A.L. VanName Jr.)

This photograph was taken in 1942 of Evelyn Mae White, at the wheel of the sailing schooner *Maggie*, and Susie Ruark, Evelyn's soon-to-be mother-in-law. A few years after this photograph, Evelyn Mae married Susie's son Talmadge, and throughout their lives they lived right beside the Ruark homestead on Jackson Creek. The women often sailed and cooked aboard the *Maggie* and *Columbia F.C.* (Courtesy of Charles A. Ruark.)

The wheel- and aft houses of the *Columbia F.C.* are in view in this photograph. When the vessel was sold, the Ruark family sat up on the hill and watched it sail away. Tom Henry forgot to take a quilt off before it left. When his wife asked him if he got her quilt off, he said, "No, and darn if I'm going after it now." (Courtesy of Dr. A.L. VanName Jr.)

Capt. David Andrew Taylor of the Eastern Shore sailed into Deltaville and met his love, Nannie Elizabeth Saunders. They were married on April 18, 1872, and made their home on Broad Creek. Captain Taylor owned the two-masted schooner *Elizabeth Ann*, the three-masted schooner *Lillie O. Wells*, and the skipjack *Nannie*. Captain Taylor was worshipful master in 1917 of Deltaville's Donovan Masonic Lodge, founded in 1887. (Courtesy of Donovan Lodge.)

The deepwater "Pot" near Jackson Creek Wharf provided for excellent anchorage of Chesapeake Bay schooners and buy boats. The Pot was close to shore and behind the banks of Mill and Jackson Creeks, which provided protection from storms. (Courtesy of William C. Hight.)

(06-852J-BF)(5-1-33-1:57P)(12-2000)   JACKSON CREEK, VA.

This 1933 aerial photograph of Mill Creek, Jackson Creek Fishing Bay, the Piankatank River, and portions of old Deltaville was taken just months before the August Storm of 1933 wiped out Jackson Creek and North End Steamboat Wharves, bringing an end to regular steamboat traffic to Deltaville. (Courtesy of Middlesex County Museum.)

Stingray Point Lighthouse was built in 1858 and served as a navigational aid until 1965, when the wooden lighthouse structure was dismantled and an automated beacon was built on its platform. Congress appropriated $250 in 1853 for a small light at Stingray Point. However, when the lighthouse was completed and went into operation on January 1, 1859, the total cost came to about $12,000. During the Civil War, the lighthouse was used as an Underground Railroad station, where Union ships picked up runaway slaves who had rowed or paddled their small crafts to freedom. Along with the beacon, the lighthouse was supplied with a fog-bell machine to strike during thick fog at alternate intervals of 5 and 30 seconds. (Courtesy of Chesapeake Bay Maritime Museum.)

Three

STEAMBOAT ERA

In 1821, the first commercial passenger steamboats to pass by Sandy Bottom were out of Norfolk, named the *Petersburg* and the *Albemarle*.

The steamers became a vital economic link between Deltaville and the cities of Baltimore, Washington, DC, Norfolk, and beyond. Commerce in Deltaville grew considerably in 1885, when Jackson Creek Wharf was built. Located at the end of Route 660, the wharf extended across Jackson Creek's channel and out into the deeper water of the Chesapeake Bay. A unique hand-operated draw was built into the wharf for small boats to come and go.

North End, or Grinels Wharf, was built in 1887 by Weems Steamboat Co. and was the first wharf to enter the river on the south side of the Rappahannock. The wharf was built at the end of what is now State Route 637 on land then owned by Southey Grinels. Unique to only North End Wharf was a stone jetty with a 40-foot-wide opening near the middle. This allowed small boats to enter and lay alongside for loading and off-loading and protection during storms.

At North End, Grinel's home Cupalow was converted to a hotel. There was a general store and United States post office named Grinels. With a busy wharf in 1912, Southey Grinels sued George W. Daniel Jr. in Middlesex County Circuit Court, to stop construction of commercial buildings and to restrain the use of existing buildings located on the wharf. According to a court injunction, Daniel's buildings were "impacting his business operation."

Conrad's Wharf was located just west of Deltaville at Woodport on the Piankatank. Prior to the construction of North End and Jackson Creek Wharves, Conrad's was a main port of call for those living near Deltaville.

Tomato- and vegetable-canning factories were located at Jackson's, North End, and Conrad's. Moight Alexander Jackson ran a country store and post office on Jackson Creek Wharf named Enoch. The wharf was occasionally called Enoch Wharf. The steamboat also frequented Ruark Wharf on Fishing Bay, operated by Capt. Al Ruark.

The steamboat carried Deltaville to the city, where youngsters witnessed their first professional baseball game, took that first ride on a roller coaster, first tasted cotton candy, and made that first trip to a department store to purchase a new "store-bought" dress. Those lasting reminders of first-time experiences were often retold again and again throughout their lives.

Jackson's Creek Wharf, Middlesex County, Va.

The Deltaville Community had steamboat service at Jackson's Wharf. The steamboats provided regular transportation for those living in Deltaville to Baltimore, Washington, DC, and Norfolk. The August Storm of 1933 destroyed Jackson Creek Wharf, and steamboat travel throughout the bay was never the same. (Courtesy of Emily Chowning.)

THE MARYLAND STEAMBOAT COMPANY.
Piers 3 and 4 Light Street.
No. *A. W. Harrow*   Baltimore, *May 10*   189*3*
To Steamer .... and owners, Dr.
For Freight on ....

Shipper.	Landing.	No. Pkgs.	Contents.
	Jacksons,	*1 Lot HH Goods*	
		1 Bale Hay	
		1 Bag Corn	
		1 Horse & Wagon	*10.40*

Received Payment, ...

This 1893 steamboat receipt shows that the Maryland Steamboat Company out of Baltimore was serving the Deltaville community. The steamboat *Avalon* arrived at "Jacksons'," as the invoice states, on May 10, 1893, bringing A.W. Harrow a bale of hay, a bag of corn, a horse and wagon and other "HH [household] goods." The *Avalon* served the Piankatank route from 1888 to 1894. (Courtesy of Willard and Shirley Norris.)

The 1888-built steamboat *Avalon* frequented Jackson Creek Wharf on a regular basis. There were two *Avalons*, and both worked the Piankatank Route. The first was built in 1882 and on September 4, 1887, burned to the water's edge at Freeport Landing, the last stop on the Piankatank River. The second *Avalon* stopped at Jackson Creek Wharf regularly until 1894, when it was moved to work Maryland's Choptank River wharves. (Courtesy of Chesapeake Bay Maritime Museum.)

This aerial photograph shows the expanse of the Chesapeake Bay in relationship to Deltaville. Jackson Creek Steamboat Wharf can be seen at the mouth of the creek. (Courtesy of Middlesex County Museum.)

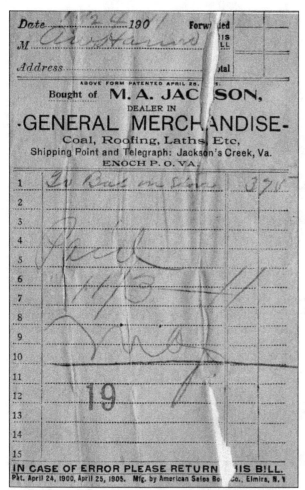

Date .... 2 .. 190   Forw[ ]ied
M .... [ ]IS
[ ]LL
Address .... [ ]tal
ABOVE FORM PATENTED APRIL 28, [ ] S.
Bought of **M. A. JAC SON,**
DEALER IN
·GENERAL MERCH ANDISE·
Coal, Roofing, Laths Etc,
Shipping Point and Telegraph: Jackson's Creek, Va.
ENOCH P. O. VA.

1		
2		
3		
4		
5		
6		
7		
8		
9		
10		
11		
12		
13		
14		
15		

IN CASE OF ERROR PLEASE RETURN IIS BILL.
Pat. April 24, 1900, April 25, 1905. Mfg. by American Sales Bo o., Elmira, N. Y

M. (Moight) Alexander Jackson was the first and only postmaster of Enoch Post Office, which started in 1885. The post office closed in 1913 but in 1911 was located in Jackson's store that was built out on Jackson Creek Steamboat Wharf. The store and wharf were blown away in the August Storm of 1933. Note that this invoice states "Enoch P.O. [post office], Va." (Courtesy of Willard and Shirley Norris.)

The Rappahannock River steamboat wharves on the south side of the river were extended far out to allow for the deepwater draft of the steamboats. North End Wharf, or Grinels Wharf, near Deltaville was the first stop on the Middlesex County side of the river. When the steamboat arrived, the wharf was abuzz with activity as those riding were often met by relatives or friends. (Courtesy of Chesapeake Bay Maritime Museum.)

The side-wheeler *Middlesex*, named after Middlesex County, Virginia, the county Deltaville is located in, served the Baltimore-to-Fredericksburg route from 1902 to 1924 and stopped regularly at North End Steamboat Wharf. The 200-foot-long vessel operated principally on the Rappahannock, Potomac, and Patuxent Rivers. (Courtesy of Judy Richwine.)

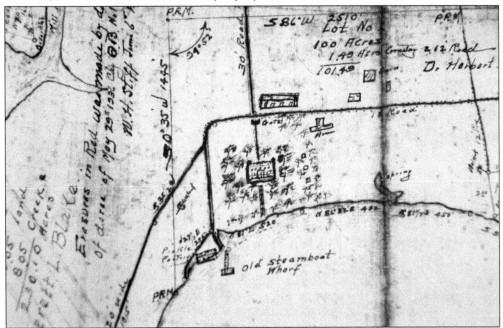

This 640-acre survey of Dr. Jno. D. Blake's property of Woodport on the Piankatank River was done January 1924 by Middlesex County surveyor Klondike Willie Stiff. It shows where the old steamboat wharf and pickle factory were located near the main house on the property. (Courtesy of Beverly and Jamie Barnhardt.)

Jackson Creek Steamboat Wharf was one of just a few wharves on Chesapeake Bay that had a draw to allow boats to enter and leave the creek. The wharf was built out over the channel and out to the deep water of Chesapeake Bay. The draw provided convenient access in and out of the creek. (Courtesy of William C. Hight.)

Four

BOATBUILDING AND BOATS

Deltaville Deadrise is a name known all over the Chesapeake Bay region. In its heyday of boatbuilding, Deltaville builders constructed wooden deadrise and cross-planked bottom boats for customers up and down the East Coast. The term *deadrise* became both a definition and the name for the style of boat.

Several things contributed to the rise of Deltaville as a boatbuilding center. In the 1890s, watermen of Sandy Bottom, as Deltaville was called in those days, used sail-powered workboats built from logs to navigate the water. The main boatbuilders then were brothers Edward and Pete Deagle, who specialized in construction and repair of boats built from logs, called log canoes.

With the introduction of internal combustion engines, bay boatbuilders began to experiment with building boats out of planks that had become more accessible at the turn of the 20th century. Basilee Cornelius and Ike Thomas are considered by some the fathers of modern boatbuilding in Deltaville. On Lovers Lane, they started building striker boats, small boats used in the menhaden fishery, out of planks. For whatever reason, the men living on that road watched and developed an uncanny interest for building planked-bottomed boats.

The introduction of the internal combustion engine in the 1890s also enhanced this new type of boat construction. Engines worked in log canoes, but boatbuilders found motors in V-shaped and cross-planked bottom boats performed better and were easier to install than in log canoes. Deltaville's "backyard boatbuilding" spread to the point that the area was considered throughout the Chesapeake Bay region the "boatbuilding capital" of wooden deadrise boats.

Deadrise is a term denoting the V shape built into the bow and bottom of the boats that when underway gives the vessel stability as it moves through choppy seas. It is the vertical distance from the chine (top of the "V"), where the bottom and side planks come together, to the keel rabbet (bottom of the "V"), where the bottom planking is nailed to the keel. The term *dead* in deadrise denotes a straight rise that forms the sides of the "V" in the bottom. The era of Deltaville's deadrise construction lasted from about 1900 into the 1990s, when the increased cost of building a wooden boat made fiberglass and steel hull boats, which required less maintenance than wood, more attractive to boat owners. However, Deltaville still retains its nickname as the "Deadrise Capital of the Chesapeake Bay."

When Deltaville's boatbuilding industry first started, boats were constructed outdoors near a large tree. The boatyard tree was used to aid in using a block and tackle to turn the completed bottom of the boat over to then work on the sides and topsides. Later on, most builders constructed their boats inside a boat shed. Capt. Hugh Norris, however, always built his skiffs and workboats in the open air. (Author's collection.)

"The Boat for All" was built by James "Jim" Bailey Cornelius, who was born in 1862 in Deltaville. Cornelius was an early boatbuilder and railway operator who lived on Jackson Creek near the public dock. Cornelius advertised his boats on a postcard and handwrote information on it to inform potential customers of his product. (Courtesy of Selden Richardson.)

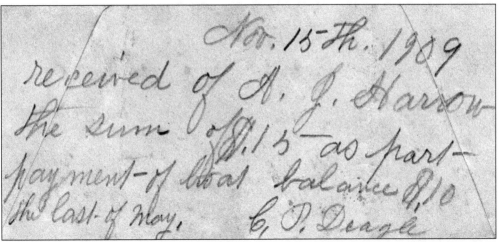

This 1909 invoice from C.P. "Pete" Deagle to Alonza Harrow for payment of "boat" was made November 15, 1909, about the time Deltaville boatbuilders began to experiment with deadrise and cross-planked construction. Deagle specialized in repair of log boats, so most likely he bought a log canoe, made repairs, and sold it to Harrow—another aspect of Deltaville boatbuilding. (Courtesy of Willard and Shirley Norris.)

Boats built out of planks became popular when local steam-powered sawmills became available to cut planks from logs. What made Deltaville's boatbuilding industry thrive were mills such as Bernard L. Wood's sawmill at Hartfield that was just a few miles west of Deltaville. When a boatbuilder needed a 12-inch-by-12-inch-by-42-foot-long keel in a hurry, "Mr. Wood always accommodated." (Courtesy of the *Southside Sentinel*.)

John Wright's boatyard on Jackson Creek was thriving when this photograph was taken in the 1930s. Captain John was considered by many to be the patriarch of wooden boatbuilding in Deltaville. He could build a 65-foot buy boat for commercial fishermen or a 12-foot skiff for a lad to putter around the creek. (Courtesy of Bob Walker.)

Lewis Wright was the son of Tom Wright, one of the early pioneers in Deltaville's deadrise construction and a nephew of John Wright. Lewis probably built as many boats as anyone in Deltaville; he was also an artist. Here he is in a 1984 photograph at his home on Jackson Creek, standing beside of his favorite painting that he did of Pres. Dwight Eisenhower. (Author's collection.)

The *Iva W.* was built in 1929 by John Wright on Jackson Creek for neighbor Capt. Johnny Ward. The *Iva W.* was named after Captain Johnny's wife, Iva (Deagle) Ward, and was worked by Captain Johnny in the winter blue crab dredge fishery for over 50 years. Today, members of the Ward family of Deltaville own several transport tugs and continue to work in the tradition of their ancestors. (Author's collection.)

Alfred Norris was one of several boatbuilders who built wooden deadrise and cross-planked boats in his backyard on Lovers Lane. Here, he is pictured by a recently completed hull at his boat shop in 1964. (Courtesy of Joe Conboy.)

Once the bottom is complete and flipped over, Alfred Norris pulls the hull outside of his shed and finishes off the rest of the boat. This photograph shows the inside stern construction of a classic Deltaville Deadrise. (Courtesy of Joe Conboy.)

Deltaville boatbuilder Grover Lee Owens was a cabinetmaker originally. When Owens was building boats, his wooden vessels were in high demand throughout the entire Chesapeake Bay region. The bottoms of Chesapeake Bay Deadrise workboats are built upside down and flipped over so the builder can complete the sides and top work. The above photograph shows Owens's hull flipped over and the side work just started. The below photograph shows the cross-planked bottom that creates the V-shaped hull and two sideboards that have been installed. The first sideboard is called a step plank and is tapered to eliminate any squareness where the bottom butts to the sides. (Both, courtesy of Thomas R. Marshall.)

This photograph shows a deadrise bottom under construction. A boatbuilding shop was a wonderful playground for a boy. There was the sweet smell of wood chips, and there was the possibility of getting a toy boat made. Capt. John Wright was known to stop work on a boat to whittle a toy boat for a lad. (Courtesy of Joe Conboy.)

The *Renell K* is a classic Deltaville Deadrise workboat that belonged to waterman Harold Kennard. The vessel was built without a pilothouse, which was standard before watermen desired their steering to be under a roof and out of the weather. (Courtesy of Joe Conboy.)

This Broad Creek round-stern deadrise also sports a round pilothouse. Deltaville's Broad Creek builders were Ed Norton; "Big" Johnny Weston; Johnny "Crab" Weston; Alvin, Moody and Raymond Walden; Linwood and Milford Price; and Paul S. Green Sr. and his sons, Paul Jr., Bobby, and Maylon. (Courtesy of Joe Conboy.)

Robert Green's father and grandfather built boats in Deltaville on Broad Creek and he learned the trade from them. He was one of the last of the Deltaville wooden deadrise builders and constructed boats into the 1990s. (Author's collection.)

One of the elements that has made the Deltaville community so appealing to recreational sailboating has been its location on Chesapeake Bay, where fair winds are almost always blowing. A sight often seen on Broad Creek are traditional workboats and recreational sailboats passing by on the waves. The wooden deadrise *Casey Jean* was built by Robert Green on Broad Creek. (Author's collection.)

As a boy, Willard Norris learned the boatbuilding trade from his uncles Alfred Norris and Lee Deagle. Norris completed the *Miss Maxine*, a wooden deadrise, in 1981 for waterman Edward Landon of Smith Island, Maryland. Norris built boats on Lovers Lane and was a Jackson Creek builder. Other Jackson Creek builders included Alfred Norris; Edmond Harrow Sr.; John, Lad, Tom, Lewis, and William E. Wright; and Bez and Jim Cornelius. (Author's collection.)

Deagle and Son Marine Railway on Fishing Bay was well known for converting commercial sailing vessels to power and for repairing of some of the largest wooden fishing vessels on the bay. Lee Deagle started his railway career by purchasing a small railway from Jim Cornelius on Jackson Creek. In 1934, he purchased Price's Boatyard and made it into one of the most successful railways on the bay. (Author's collection.)

The repair and maintenance of wooden boats has been an important part of Deltaville's economy. Some of the largest vessels on Chesapeake Bay were worked on at Deagle and Son Marine Railway. Here, a worker is repairing the bottom of the *Bugeye O.A. Bloxom*, a ship measuring 75 feet, by 21 feet, by 4.5 feet. It was converted to power at Deagle's in 1949. Lee Deagle and his son Ed ran the business for over 50 years. (Author's collection.)

The *Jo-El II* was built in Deltaville at Price's Railway in 1955 for Charles W. Krumen-Acker of New York City. The boat was used for charter fishing and cruises during the winter in West Palm Beach, Florida, and during the summer in Long Island. All types of wooden boats were built by Deltaville builders and sold to customers up and down the East Coast. (Courtesy of Joe Conboy.)

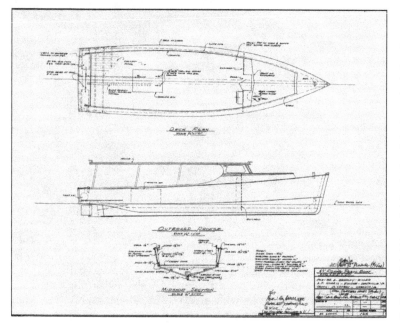

This line drawing of a 42-foot fishing-party boat built for Bradley Miller is unusual in that there are few drawn plans of Deltaville boats. Most builders worked by what they called "rake of eye," meaning they had no drawings or plans. Running fishing parties to hook and line fish was another aspect of the community's economy. (Courtesy of Joe Conboy.)

John Collamore III moved to Deltaville in 1972 from Rhode Island and opened Hulls Unlimited East Inc., a fiberglass-boatbuilding shop in town. Collamore and Whitey Laurier and Arthur L. Helbig of Gloucester County were Virginia pioneers in fiberglass-workboat building. Collamore and boat designer Harry Bulifont introduced the Deltaville Garvey as one of several styles of vessels that he built and marketed. The *Defender* was a garvey built to put out fires. (Both, author's collection.)

In 1982, Coddie Carrington and John Fowler combined the traditional shape of the Deltaville Deadrise and built a Bay Deadrise out of aluminum. Their company Delta Marine was one of the first to build a deadrise-style boat out of aluminum. The boat was made in a boatbuilding shed located on the road that once led to North End Steamboat Wharf. (Author's collection.)

In July 1983, Bryan Miller of Miller Marine Railway launched this aluminum lobster boat on Broad Creek for a New England fisherman. Miller is the grandson of Lee Deagle and son of Virgil Miller, both well-known boatbuilders in the Deltaville Community. By 1983, wood was no longer the only material used to build boats there. (Author's collection.)

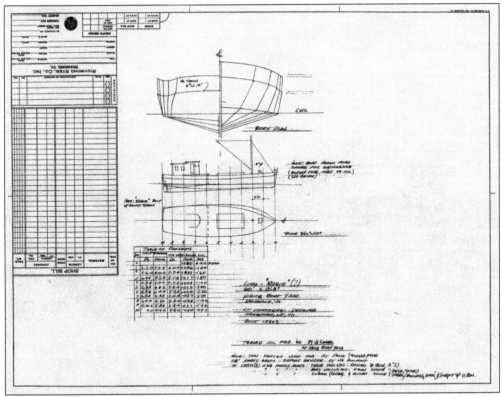

Most Deltaville boatbuilders seldom used plans. Linwood and Milford Price were builders who built from "rack of eye," but also on occasion used boat plans drawn by naval architects. The 60-foot-by-13-foot-8-inches buy boat *Marie* was built at Price's Boatyard in 1950. The plans show a square stern on the boat, but the Prices added their own touch by installing a round stern. (Courtesy of Joe Conboy.)

This 80-foot-by-24-foot steel-hull ferryboat, built for the Tidewater Transportation District of the Virginia Department of Highway, was constructed in Deltaville in 1986 by Miller's Marine Railway. The vessel was certified to carry 150 passengers and exemplified the diversity at that time of the boatbuilding industry in the community. (Author's collection.)

Built in Deltaville, the lobster boat *Rachel Leah* is featured in an August 2007 episode of *Lobster Wars*, a documentary television series on the Discovery Channel about lobstering off the George's Bank. This photograph shows the boat on its maiden launch in 1988 at Deagle and Son Marine Railway on Fishing Bay. It was built by Byran Miller of Miller Marine Railway for Bob Brown, who would became famous a decade or so later as the owner of the *Andrea Gail*, the trawler that got caught in the Perfect Storm of 1991. The movie *The Perfect Storm* premiered in 2000 and is based on a 1997 book written by Sebastian Junger. (Author's collection.)

Five

COMMERCE

During the colonial years, Deltaville's commerce was centered on the growing of tobacco. Kemp's Landing, which was in the vicinity of Wilton Creek, had a warehouse and custom facility that handled the distribution of tobacco in the area. A reminder of that time is Tobacco Cove, located at the mouth of Jackson Creek and nestled against Stove Point, with its name passed down from bygone days. After the Revolution, the tobacco culture began to wane and Deltaville turned its commercial efforts towards the sea.

The location of Deltaville between two rivers and Chesapeake Bay provided economic diversity for the area. The Rappahannock and Piankatank were prime rivers for harvesting oysters; both rivers and Chesapeake Bay were good for harvesting finfish and crabs.

As earnings from the water increased, retail commerce in and around Deltaville began to grow. Country stores and other land-operated commercial endeavors began to emerge. Marine railways provided jobs to build and maintain boats used in the fishing industry. The hauling of freight and agriculture products by water also stimulated the local economy. Agriculture grew as steam-operated canning factories processed tomatoes, peas, and other vegetables. Deltaville's rich soil was ideal for growing watermelons, cantaloupes, and other fruits and vegetables. The steamboat and freight boats owned by Deltaville families enabled these products to be transported to a city market.

Towards the end of the 1920s, vacationing and recreational boating began to become an important part of Deltaville's economy. Richmond church groups scheduled Sunday school bus trips to Deltaville. A Saturday out on the water hook-and-line fishing on local charter boats concluded with dinner at Taylor's Restaurant. People also began to come down and rent cottages, and as they became familiar with the wonderful waterfront environment, many decided to purchase summer homes and boats. The bay attracted those who loved to sail, and many people arrived by sailboat to enjoy the fair winds off Deltaville's shores. Others stopped by to purchase needed supplies for their journeys.

The water and sea have always been prime ingredients in the economic life of Deltaville. Whether the occupation has been sailor, sailmaker, boatbuilder, freighter, fisherman, marina owner, or railway man, the community's commerce has always stemmed from its advantageous location near the Chesapeake Bay.

S.J. "Sammy" Moore's store in Sandy Bottom was the largest general merchandise store in the area. Moore was a successful businessman who was also involved in banking. Moore and Maj. Parker Grinels of Wake established the first official bank in the area, known as Packers State Bank. The bank was formed in 1920 to accommodate a growing economy created by the vegetable and oyster packing businesses. (Courtesy of Middlesex County Public Library.)

On the back of this photograph of an early blacksmith shop in Deltaville is written, "Mr. Ernest Fox and Roland Evans at blacksmith shop." The building was owned by Ed Bristow, who had a smithy shop inside and also stored wooden caskets for sale. Over time, E.W. Bristow & Son Funeral Directors became the center of their business. The family also ran a jitney service. (Courtesy of Hugh and Dorothy Norris.)

When W.H. Carter ran a general merchandise store in the Sandy Bottom community, there were country stores on most every crossroad. Although no one interviewed recalls the store being in operation, or Carter, his store's letterhead establishes that it did indeed exist prior to 1900. The store sold dry goods, notions, shoes, hats, caps, rubber goods, jewelry, and, as a specialty, offered watch repair. (Courtesy of Willard and Shirley Norris.)

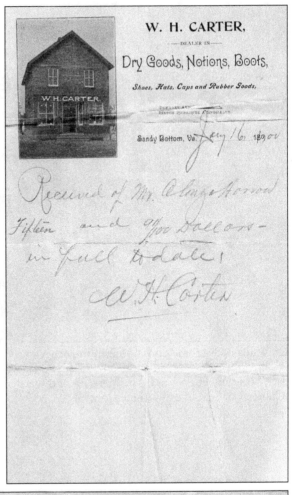

Deltaville's Sammy Moore was cofounder in 1920 of Packers State Bank in Wake, where most of the people living in the eastern end of Middlesex County did their banking. Jesse (Norton) Hurd Jr. of Deltaville received this Packers State Bank check in 1924 from A.W. Harrow. (Courtesy of Willard and Shirley Norris.)

Dr. William Gwathmey, on the left in the buggy, traveled to patients by horse and buggy, motor-powered log canoe, or, when Deltaville dirt roads were passable, Ford Model T. For the most part, horse and buggy was his main means of travel. Paved roads were still a ways into the future. (Courtesy of Caroline Gwathmey Jones.)

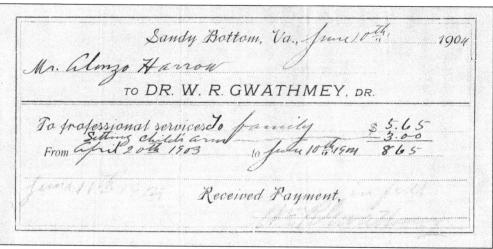

Dr. William R. Gwathmey, who was the family physician for Sandy Bottom in 1903, set a broken arm for Alonza Harrow's child and charged $3 for the service. Dr. Gwathmey of King & Queen County moved to Ruark around 1900 and set up his practice. (Courtesy of Willard and Shirley Norris.)

HOTEL SAMORE, STINGRAY POINT, DELTAVILLE, VA.

This 1938 postcard shows Hotel Samore at Stingray Point, owned by Sammy Moore and named for him. Deltaville's location right on Chesapeake Bay, and between the Rappahannock and Piankatank Rivers, made the community an ideal warm-weather spot for sailing, recreational fishing, swimming, walking along the beach, and catching a summer breeze off Chesapeake Bay. When the hotel burned, Stingray Point Hotel replaced it. (Courtesy of Emily Chowning.)

This photograph, taken around 1939 in a snowstorm near the corner of Lovers Lane and the main road, shows that businesses were growing in the center of town. Boaters and summer visitors were already making their way there, but in the cold-weather months there was a warm feeling of home as the community was left to those who lived there year-round. (Courtesy of Betsy Hudgins.)

Oysters and seafood harvested from local waters were a big part of the local economy for many years. North End Steamboat Wharf and Jackson Creek Wharf had oyster storage houses built right out on the wharves, and steamboats provided a city market for Rappahannock and Piankatank River oysters. In 1965, the harvesting of oysters was good, and these oystermen, working hand oyster tongs, are tonging at the mouth of the Piankatank. (Courtesy of John M. Bareford Jr.)

The *Blanch E*, a deadrise workboat out of Locklies Creek, is on the Piankatank oyster grounds in 1965 as two tongers, Bradley Miller and Lawrence Jones, work to fill the boat with seed oysters. Oysters were caught and sold on oyster grounds to Capt. Johnny Ward of Deltaville in his oyster buy boat the *Iva W.* (Courtesy of John M. Bareford Jr.)

This photograph shows the buy boat *Iva W.*, owned by Capt. Johnny Ward of Deltaville, as Ward buys seed oysters in the Piankatank River just off Fishing Bay from oystermen catching oysters with hand tongs. The boat looks to be just about loaded. (Courtesy of John M. Bareford Jr.)

Starting in the 1850s, the oyster business became an important aspect of Deltaville's economy. It provided wintertime work for families who depended on the water for their sustenance. The tub of oysters in the bottom of this deadrise boat is being sold to a Deltaville buy boat. The oystermen are Hughes (left) and Leroy Nelson of Remlik. (Courtesy of John M. Bareford Jr.)

Capt. R.D. Ailsworth, atop the pilothouse, is keeping tally on the bushel tubs of oysters that are coming aboard his oyster buy boat the *Lillian T.* Captain Ailsworth and crew could buy oysters from four deadrise oyster boats at a time. The tallyman had to keep count of the number of bushels and from which boat each one came. The 55-foot *Lillian T.* was built by Linwood Price of Deltaville in 1928. (Courtesy of Alfred E. Ailsworth Jr.)

Dredging for winter blue crabs was outlawed by the Virginia Marine Resources Commission in 2008. Prior to that year, Deltaville watermen worked annually in the Chesapeake Bay's winter crab dredge fishery. Pictured here are two crabbing dredge boats, the *Iva W.* and *Muriel Eileen*, at home on Jackson Creek. (Courtesy of Capt. Johnny Ward.)

Capt. Johnny Ward and his sons, Floyd, Melvin and Milton, all of Deltaville, worked in the winter crab dredge fishery and owned several of the largest wooden boats in the region. This photograph of the *Ward Bros.* was taken in 1985. (Author's collection.)

Capt. Floyd Ward gets ready to off-load a barrel of crabs from his father's boat, the *Iva W.*, onto the *Ward Bros.* Deltaville watermen have worked in Virginia's winter crab dredge fishery for over 100 years. (Author's collection.)

Working the water is as much a part of Deltaville's heritage as boatbuilding. Gywnn's Island in Mathews County and Deltaville are just a few miles apart by water. In the 1980s, Deltaville crabbers bought menhaden to bait their crab pots from pound netter Wilson Rowe (in the skiff). Rowe's net was right off Gywnn's Island, and the morning ritual of Deltaville crabbers was to head towards his net to buy bait. (Author's collection.)

AGREEMENT.

THIS AGREEMENT made this ___ day of _Apr_ 19_12_ between _____ _Mr A. W. Harrow_, party of the first part, and the Daniel Packing Co., party of the second part, witnesseth that the said party of the first part, agrees to sell and deliver to said Daniel Packing Co. at their cannery at Amburg, Va., all the marketable tomatoes grown on _2½_ acres of land, to be planted by the said party of the first part during the season of 19_ _ the said tomatoes to be delivered red ripe and in such size and merchantable order as the said Daniel Packing Co. shall require, (otherwise the said Daniel Packing Co. shall not be required to receive and pay for any tomatoes,) and the party of the first part agrees to use baskets or _____ of tomatoes for a good quality. _10 × 14 × 24 long_

In consideration, _____ the said Daniel Packing Co., do hereby covenant and agree to pay to the said party of _____ part the sum of _25_ cts. per _____ for tomatoes delivered as aforesaid, payments to be the _____ of _____ and _____. No tomatoes to be received on Saturday, except such as the parties of the second part may be able to handle on that day.

In witness whereof the said parties have hereunto set their hands the day and year aforesaid.

DANIEL PACKING CO.

The Daniel family operated a vegetable-canning house under the name Daniel Packing Co. and in 1912 required signed agreements between growers and the company. A.W. Harrow, who lived on Lovers Lane, contracted to plant 2.5 acres worth of tomatoes on his land near his home and was paid 25¢ a bushel. They had to be of good quality and packaged in 10-by-14-by-24-inch boxes or in bushel baskets. (Courtesy of Willard and Shirley Norris.)

A tomato-picking crew is picking tomatoes in the August heat for Delta Canning Company of Deltaville. The company was the last tomato-canning factory in Deltaville. It closed in 1970. Tomato canning was a big part of the economy of the Deltaville community for many years. (Courtesy of the *Southside Sentinel*.)

Pride of the Redskin Brand tomatoes were sold and distributed by Delta Canning Co. The Daniel family owned the cannery for many years. In the 1950s, Earl Daniel sold the company to a Pennsylvania firm. James Crittenden purchased the business in the early 1960s and continued to use the label. The company closed in 1970, ending a long era of vegetable and fruit canning. (Courtesy of Tyler Crittenden.)

Iona tomatoes were a brand name for the Great Atlantic & Pacific Tea Company out of New York. Iona tomatoes were one of four brands canned by Delta Canning Co. in Deltaville. The others were Red-Glo and Pine Cone for Albert W. Sisk and Son, Inc. out of Aberdeen, Maryland, and Pride of the Redskin, the local brand of the company when owned by James Crittenden. (Courtesy of Tyler Crittenden.)

Deltaville-built freight boats were used up and down the Chesapeake Bay, but one group that utilized them as much as any were the watermen of Tangier Island, Virginia. Pictured here on Tangier are, from left to right, *Nellie Jane*, built by Deltaville boatbuilder Buddy Sable in 1939; and *Joyce Sterling* and *Ruth S.*, both built by at Linwood Price's Deltaville boatyard in 1930 and 1927 respectively. (Courtesy of William C. Hight.)

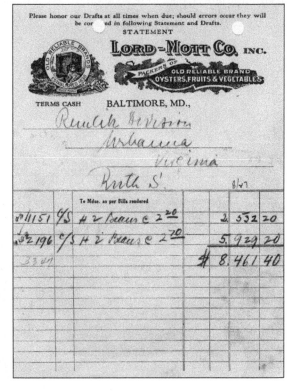

This August 1927 Lord-Mott Co. Inc. of Baltimore, Maryland, invoice states that beans were shipped to Lord-Mott's Remlik Division in Urbanna on the *Ruth S*. This very well may have been Deltaville captain Johnny Stiff's first commercial trip in his new wooden buy boat. Stiff had local boatbuilder Linwood Price build him a 60.3-by-17.7-by-5.7-foot wooden boat in 1927 to haul freight and grain and to buy oysters. (Courtesy of William C. Hight.)

After World War II, recreational activities along the waters of the Chesapeake Bay began to expand as recreational boating and fishing inspired relaxation and sport. Deltaville was in a prime location to capitalize on this. In the early 1950s, Edwin and Dorothea Conger of Staunton bought the property at Horse Point on the Piankatank and Healy Creek and built and operated Horse Point Inn and motel. (Courtesy of Billy and Mabel Williams.)

Hook and line fishing and recreational sailing out of Broad and Jackson Creeks and Fishing Bay began to boost the economy. Fisherman trolled the Rappahannock or Piankatank Rivers or Chesapeake Bay, catching a variety of species. This fishermen standing on Ed Norton's dock on Broad Creek obviously had a pretty good day, having caught a good-size red drum. (Courtesy of Carolyn Norton Schmalenberger.)

Although extremely busy creeks, Jackson and Board Creeks require dredging more frequently than most creeks in the region as wind and tide cause shifting sand on the bottoms. This photograph was taken September 1964 of a dredge/pile driver rig dredging near the mouth of Jackson Creek. (Courtesy of Joe Conboy.)

William Healy Stiff of Deltaville was a colorful character who lived in a cottage on Stove Point. Known to most as "Klondike Willie," he was born in 1874 and his family gave him the nickname of Willie, but Klondike came from his adventures in the 1896 Alaskan gold rush. He later obtained his surveying credentials and came home in 1915 to start a surveying business. (Courtesy of Emily Chowning.)

Mr Raymond Blake
Harmony Village, Va

In Account With

W. H. Stiff
Civil Engineer
Certified Surveyor No. 147
Deltaville, Va.

J. K. Sinclair
Certified Surveyor
Gloucester, Va.
PHONE: GLOUCESTER 3-2551

1964

March 26 | To Survey with Maps & Blue Prints | $18.00

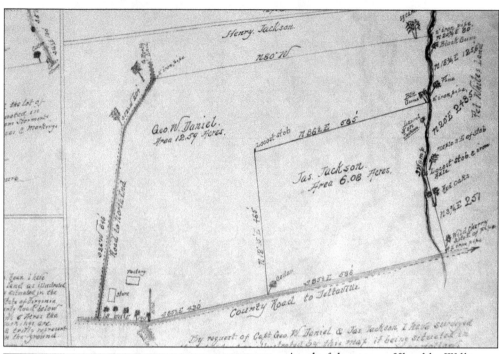

A colorful surveyor, Klondike Willie Stiff often left his mark on his drawings. On this one, which shows the "County Road to Deltaville," he points out the "Road to North End" steamboat landing, George Daniel's tomato-canning factory, and a store on the corner. (Courtesy of Middlesex County Clerk's Office.)

HARDYVILLE, VA.,	August 11	1952

M Lord Mott Packing Co.

Urbanna, Virginia

IN ACCOUNT WITH

CRITTENDEN MOTOR LINES

GENERAL HAULING

PHONE: DELTA 3700

6-26	200 bags insecticides from		
	Planters Chem. 10000# @.30	$ 30.00	
	Tax	.90	
		$ 30.90	

Shortly after World War II, the freight business in Deltaville began to shift away from using boats to hauling bulk product in trucks. Crittenden Motor Lines in Hardyville, just a short distance west of Deltaville, was one of several freight lines that emerged with the rise of good roads and dependable trucks. (Courtesy of William C. Hight.)

The better roads also brought more people to the community and helped boost retail business. Norton Hurd of Hurd's Hardware had already ordered his riding lawn mowers for spring when a late snowstorm hit Deltaville in March 1970. The store today is one of the busiest in Middlesex County. (Courtesy of the *Southside Sentinel.*)

The Bank of Middlesex received a charter for general banking in December 1900. That year, the bank started in the town of Urbanna. A branch was opened in Saluda in 1911, and nearly 50 years later in 1964, a Deltaville branch opened, a sign that the community was growing. The bank stayed locally owned until December 1985, when it merged with First Virginia. (Courtesy of John M. Bareford Jr.)

After Sam Moore's hotel, Samore, burned on Stingray Point, Eddie Harrow built Stingray Point Hotel. During the early years, its was painted white, but it was later painted red and became known as the Old Red Barn. The hotel featured a duckpin bowling alley, a restaurant with fine food, and the delight of being right on Chesapeake Bay for visitors to swim, fish, and sail. (Courtesy of Edmond Harrow Jr.)

The John Andrew Twigg Bridge across the Piankatank River was just about complete when this photograph was taken in August 1953. Efforts to get the bridge built resulted in the formation of the Deltaville Improvement Association (DIA), which has become a driving force towards positive growth and development in the Deltaville community. The bridge replaced a ferry. (Courtesy of Dick Murray.)

Six

EDUCATION

As part of the federal reconstruction of the South in 1871, some 11 one-room, public-funded, segregated elementary schools were built in Middlesex County, in which Deltaville is located.

By 1891, the number of public elementary school buildings in Middlesex had increased to 28. One of those county schools was the Dunbar Graded School in Amburg (now Deltaville), built in 1886 to educate black children.

In Sandy Bottom, Rev. Charles Read Moses founded a private secondary school in 1895 known as Delta Academy for white children. Students were taught English, literature, Latin, French, German, mathematics, moral science, natural science, history, composition, physiology, hygiene, and penmanship.

The year 1907 was a landmark year for education in Deltaville, as Unionville High School, the first public high school in Middlesex County, was founded.

Students from first to eleventh grades were taught there, and it was the first school in the area to reach state secondary education accreditation in the 1912–1913 school sessions. This school drew many out-of-county students, who boarded in Deltaville to attend high school. The last graduating class from Unionville was in 1924. After that, students seeking a diploma had to finish their educations at the accredited Syringa High School, about eight miles away. The Unionville building continued to be used as Deltaville Grade School until 1962, when Deltaville and Syringa schools consolidated to create Wilton Elementary School, located several miles west of Deltaville. Syringa High School was consolidated with Saluda High School in 1950, creating Middlesex High School (MHS) in Saluda.

After 1962, the area's white children received their elementary education at Wilton and secondary education at MHS, a 20-mile commute for those living in Deltaville. Dunbar School closed in 1962 when a new all-black elementary school was built for all the black children in the county. In 1969, Middlesex schools were totally integrated, and black and white students attended the same schools.

Deltaville School 1919

Unionville High School at Sandy Bottom, now Deltaville, was the first public secondary school in Middlesex County. It was also the first state-accredited high school. Opening ceremonies were held on July 4, 1907. The public school ended what was called the academy era, when privately owned academies were the only means of secondary schooling. (Courtesy of Middlesex County Museum.)

This 1897 report card of Miss Callie Vaughan shows that Delta Academy, run by principal Rev. C. Read Moses, had students taking rather rigorous classes. Private academies went back to colonial times in the Deltaville area, and Delta Academy was one of the last to operate in the area as public schools took their place. (Courtesy of Deltaville Maritime Museum.)

Virginia Ward (left), Dorathy Norris, and Norton Hurd all attended Unionville School in Deltaville. The cornerstone and handbell that were part of the school are in the foreground. Embossed on the side of the cornerstone are names of the original trustees—W.H. Norton, E.S. Vaughn, and Granville H. Walker. (Courtesy of the *Southside Sentinel*.)

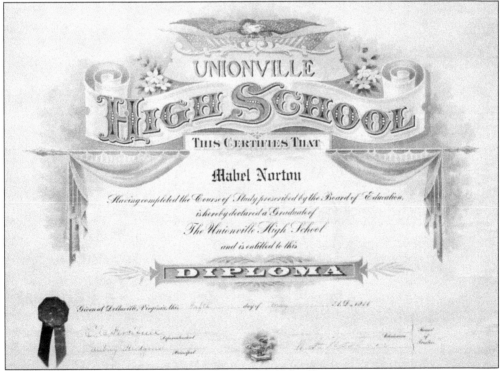

This Unionville High School diploma was awarded to Mabel Norton in 1911, the fifth year that the school was open. The school was one of just a few public school high schools in the region and students came from surrounding counties to attend and boarded in homes of Deltaville families. (Courtesy of Middlesex County Museum.)

The playground at Deltaville school was a place boys and girls learned to play and to get along with one another. Whether of football or tag, memories of childhood often travel back to days of playing on the schoolyard. (Courtesy of Alfred E. Ailsworth Jr.)

After the Civil War, part of the Federal reconstruction of Middlesex County and Deltaville was to establish free segregated schools for blacks and whites. A one-room school was erected for black children in 1886 in Amburg, now Deltaville, and named Dunbar Graded School. In 1915, the school was enlarged to four rooms and was completed with funds donated by members of Clarksbury Methodist Church, an all-white congregation. (Courtesy of George Robinson.)

Members of Deltaville's 1937 second-grade class are, from left to right, (first row) Paul Foster, Warren Selby, Milton Ward, Dickie Taylor, and Lewis Shreeves; (second row) Marvin Benson, Willard Norris, Ed Crittenden, James Raynor Ailsworth, and Charlie Fetterolf; (third row) Garland Douglas, Apple Ailsworth, Lewis Benson, Bobby Jackson, Raynell Kennard, Nelda Prince, Shirley Harrow, Mary Johnson, Raynell Yates, Ben Fetterolf, Bennie Foster, Henry Jackson, and Harold Shreeves; (fourth row) Leland Marchant, Thelma Walden, Ann Walden, Mae Vaughan, and Laura Weston; and (fifth row) Sally Callis, Myrtle Deagle, Mrs. Spencer, and Julia Wray Hall. (Courtesy of Willard and Shirley Norris.)

The above photograph is of the 1937 seventh-grade class and the image below is of the eighth- and ninth-grade classes at Deltaville School. By then, the school safety-patrol program for older students was in place, as seen in the student on the second row in the image below, who is wearing his patrol badge. The "Me" in that photograph is Margaret Moffitt (Robins). (Courtesy of Betsy Hudgins and Garland Robins.)

Some members of the 1936–1937 Deltaville High School baseball team are Winfred Hall, Norman Hall, Steven Harrow, Talmadge Ruark, Bernard Selby, and William Fox; the coach was principal Paul Topping, who is standing in the back. (Courtesy of Norman Hall.)

The 1950s May Day Court sits on stage at Deltaville School, watching the festivities of the day. May Day was an annual event at the school where everyone was encouraged to participate and the community came out in support. The May Court and Maypole Dance were the highlights of the day. (Courtesy of Garland Robins.)

The Maypole Dance was a part of the annual festivities and had been since the school was founded. In this photograph, it appears that the girls get a chance to dance around the maypole without the boys. (Courtesy of Garland Robins.)

This photograph shows the emergency fire escape on the side of the building and provides an overview of the May Day program. Along with dance, song was part of the day as an upright piano was brought out on the lawn and children sang to the music. (Courtesy of Garland Robins.)

Velma (Norton) Glasco, left, stands with some friends at the Deltaville School in 1939. Note there are two steeples on the school as a bell tower was added to the original building. (Courtesy of Betsy Hudgins.)

Schoolmates at Deltaville School in the 1930s gather outside a window of the school building to get their picture taken as several people watch from inside through the window. The citizens of Deltaville were forerunners in providing a strong form of education to their children, as they seemed to understand early on that education brightens everyone's future. (Courtesy of Garland Robins.)

The 1945 graduating glass of Syringa High School included Deltaville students. Pictured are, from left to right, (first row) Floyd Ward, Shirley Harrow, Mary Ruth Johnson, Ida Miller, Frances Nunley, Julia Thomas, Julia Wray Hall, and principal Stanley Armstead; (second row) Howard Crittenden, Hyacinth Hurley, Laura Weston, Estelle Mason, Hyacinth Major, and Julian Selby; (third row) Alvin Norton, Christian Willaford, Syd Thrift, James Harrow, Turner Blake, Elwood Johnson, and Games Dozier. (Courtesy of Willard and Shirley Norris.)

Seven

RELIGION

Permanent settlement of the English in Middlesex County and Deltaville started in 1649. When the first Englishmen settled there, they established the church of the Virginia Colony with the Church of England, also known as the Anglican Church.

An Anglican frame-structure church named Lower Church was built in 1657, and a brick church, still standing today, was completed in a year now unknown. Those living in the Deltaville area were required by English law to attend that church or they were fined. In 1666, Lower Church became a "chapel of ease" and Christ Church, towards the middle of the county, became the main church for everyone living in Middlesex.

Although Deltaville citizens continued to attend the chapel at Lower, the countywide business of running the church was handled at Christ Church. The Anglican Church was the required church until after the American Revolution, when the spread of the so-called Great Awakening brought Baptist, Methodist, and other religious groups to Deltaville. They formed their own churches in the area.

Zoar Baptist Church was constituted on November 4, 1808, when a group of predominately black and a small number of white citizens broke away from Hermitage Baptist Church in Church View to form Zoar.

Clarksbury United Methodist Church was built in 1839 in the Amburg area of Deltaville. Church records state the church was "very much injured by the soldiers during the Civil War and rendered unfit for service." It was repaired and is still in service today.

Philippi Christian Church was organized in 1871. The first structure was built at Wake, but after a fire in 1880 destroyed the building, a new church was constructed in the heart of Deltaville.

The only all-black church in Deltaville is First Baptist of Amburg, founded by a group of citizens who decided in 1867 to break away from Zoar Baptist Church and start their own church.

One of the most dynamic religious movements came to Deltaville in 1908 when the Middlesex Holiness Association organized and began to hold annual camp meetings at the Tabernacle. The group appears to have had earlier ties to Union Church, which was a nondenominational church established by Col. Moses Boss in Sandy Bottom. At the tabernacle, a sinner could be saved on the sawdust floor, and that was one of the attractions—instant salvation!

Permanent English settlement began in the Deltaville area in 1649, which was then part of Lancaster County. The established church was the Church of England, also known as the Anglican Church. Those living in what would become Deltaville helped establish Lower Church, part of the Peanckatanck Parish, and were required by law to attend and give to the church regularly. (Courtesy of Betty Chowning.)

Christ Church Parish was formed from Lancaster and Piankatank Parishes in 1666 and Christ Church became the mother church of Middlesex County, which included the far eastern end of the county that became Deltaville. Those settlers living in the eastern end mostly attended Lower Church for worship on the Sabbath, but were often required to travel to the mother church for worship and church business. (Courtesy of Betty Chowning.)

The Baptist movement was part of America's Great Awakening that came to Middlesex County in 1771. Glebe Landing Baptist is the mother church of Middlesex, while Hermitage Baptist is its daughter church. The granddaughter church is Zoar Baptist, founded November 4, 1808, out of Hermitage. This drawing is of an early Zoar Church building long gone. Zoar has grown to be one of the largest church families in the community. (Courtesy of Zoar Baptist Church.)

First Baptist of Amburg was originally part of Zoar Baptist Church. After the Civil War in 1867, Zoar's black members decided to organize their own church and First Baptist of Amburg was formed. This church photograph is of the structure that stands today and was built in 1901 after the original church building burned in 1895. (Courtesy of First Baptist of Amburg.)

Clarksbury United Methodist Church was founded in the 1830s. The "bury" in Clarksbury is for Francis Asbury, America's first Methodist bishop, who came to Middlesex around 1800 to spread the word of Methodism. The "Clark" is for Adam Clark, who was part of the early Methodist movement in England. During the Civil War, Company B of the Confederate 109th Virginia Militia mustered on the church lawn. (Courtesy of John M. Bareford Jr.)

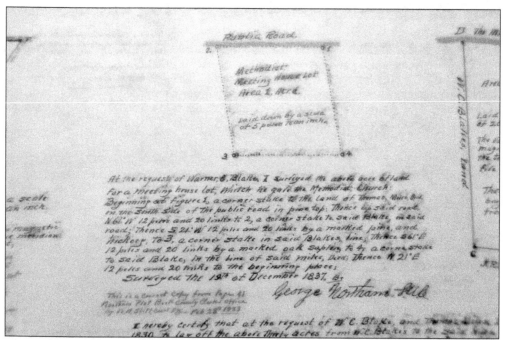

This December 19, 1837, survey of the Methodist Meeting House Lot relates the early movement of Methodism into the area. Clarksbury Methodist Church was built on this land in 1839. The building suffered from ill use during the Civil War. The trustees noted in October 30, 1866, that "the church was very much injured by the soldiers during the war and was rendered unfit for worship." (Courtesy of Middlesex County Clerk's Office.)

Officials taking part in a 1965 dedication of a new addition at Clarksbury United Methodist Church are, from left to right, (front row) L.G. Gemmill, trustee; Milford F. Price, lay leader; Dr. H. Bernard Lipscomb Jr., superintendent of Rappahannock District; and Harry C. Renner, pastor; (back row) H. Ermont Willaford, chairman of the board; H.W. Glenn Jr., trustee; T.H. Crittenden, chairman of trustees; and Fred Crittenden, chairman of education. (Courtesy of John M. Bareford Jr.)

This photograph shows Philippi Christian Church before the open bell tower was installed after a tornado in April 2011 damaged the 1885 church structure. The original building had neither steeple nor vestibule, which were added in 1914; Sunday school rooms were built in 1940 and 1954. The church was organized in 1871. (Courtesy of Middlesex County Museum.)

There was a centennial cake-cutting celebration at Philippi Christian Church in August 1971. Rev. David Brown, pastor of Philippi, and senior ladies of the church cut the cake. Maud Hurd (left), Blanche Wright (center), and Mary Evans help the minster. (Courtesy of the *Southside Sentinel*.)

One of the most dynamic religious figures in the history of Deltaville and Middlesex County was Rev. Edwin J. Moffitt, who, along with others, brought the Holiness movement to the area. Moffitt and his family lived in Deltaville. (Courtesy of Garland Robins.)

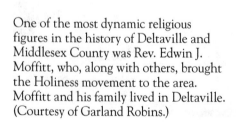

Vacation Bible School at Zoar Baptist was a special place in the 1950s for these youngsters. The churches of Deltaville have faithfully spread the word of God and brought spiritual strength, comfort, and joy to the community. (Courtesy of Willard and Shirley Norris.)

This photograph was taken in 1967 of the congregation of First Baptist of Amburg. The church was originally a spiritual home for former slaves who wanted their own special meeting place. Sitting in front is Rev. W.E. Payne, pastor of the church for 45 years. (Courtesy of First Baptist of Amburg.)

The Holiness movement came to Deltaville when minister Edwin J. Moffitt founded the Middlesex Holiness Association on November 27, 1909. The first trustees of the church were J.H. Norton, K.C. Yates, George Kellum, and E.D. Moore. The group built a chapel (pictured), and the Tabernacle, an outside pavilion that held about one thousand people. (Courtesy of Garland Robins.)

Holiness Camp meetings were held throughout the area and this group, some of whose members were from Deltaville, was at a camp meeting in Dutton in the 1930s. Reverend Moffitt, standing to the left in a bow tie, was a hell-fire-and-damnation preacher who offered salvation to those interested in accepting Christ at these religious awakening camps. (Courtesy of Garland Robins.)

Eight

PEOPLE

The greatest strength of any community lies within the hearts and souls of its people. It has been the people of Deltaville who have made it a special place.

Determination and grit have been most evident in the personality of the Deltaville community. When Unionville High School was built in 1907, very little public tax money was available or offered for the construction project. The community banded together to collect funds for the first public high school in Middlesex County. People like Addie Harrow sold her cow to put money towards the school.

The concrete John Andrew Twigg Bridge across the Piankatank River was completed in 1953, largely due to the efforts starting around 1945 of a newly formed group, the Deltaville Improvement Association. Led by Jerry Harrow, the DIA worked tirelessly to support the construction of a bridge across the Piankatank, thus ending generations of ferryboat rides and boosting commerce in Deltaville.

The community also had individuals who went off to make a difference in the world beyond. Sam Jackson, born in 1860, left Deltaville and settled in Oregon, where he later founded the Portland newspaper the *Oregon Journal*. James Raynor Ailsworth grew up in Deltaville in the 1930s and 1940s, went off to Hollywood to found the James Ellsworth Productions studios, and was a pioneer in film productions. He produced Johnny Cash's first motion picture, *Five Minutes to Live*.

Wars brought out Deltaville's heroes as well. Lt. William "Billy" S. Marchant flew a P-47 Thunderbolt fighter plane near Rennes, France, crashed in a field, and was killed. In 1985, the Combat Veterans of Foreign Wars Post 9636 dedicated a plaque and marker in his honor in front of the Deltaville Community Center. Another Deltaville pilot, Norton Hurd, was awarded the Distinguished Flying Cross from the Navy after shooting down several Japanese airplanes and crash landing in the Pacific Ocean. Raymond Burrell was a member of the African American 761st Tank Battalion of Gen. George S. Patton's Third Army that saw extensive action at the Battle of the Bulge in the winter of 1944–1945. The famous baseball star Jackie Robinson bunked three bunks down from Burrell and they often talked.

Fame and fortune, however, are not the main ingredients of the people of Deltaville. The strength of the community lies in its heritage of the sea and a tradition of understanding the necessities of life.

Sandy Bottom, Virginia, was home to Bettye & Blythe Photographics, as the embossment on this photograph reveals. With its location on the end of the Middle Peninsula and waterways being the main highway of those times, Deltaville provided an advantageous location for various commercial endeavors for people coming and going on steamboats and sailing vessels. (Author's collection.)

Embossed on the back of this old photograph of a young child is "J.J. Jackson, Amburg, Va." It is unclear whether or not this is J.J. as a child. Most likely, the photograph was taken by a traveling photographer who used Jackson's General Merchandise Store at New Market as a studio. (Author's collection.)

United States Air Force lieutenant William "Billy" S. Marchant of Deltaville was killed June 10, 1944, in World War II while flying a P-47 Thunderbolt fighter plane near Rennes, France, that crashed in a field. His body is buried at Brittany American Cemetery near Saint-James, Manche, France. In the photograph below, Lieutenant Marchant is receiving honors for courage in battle. (Both, courtesy of Frances Marchant Hall.)

In the winter of 1944–1945, Raymond W. Burrell was fighting with the now famous segregated Black Panthers of the 761st Tank Battalion who saw extensive action at the Battle of the Bulge, Hitler's last desperate effort to stop the Allies. The 761st was the first African American tank battalion. The famous baseball star Jackie Robinson was in the battalion and slept three bunks down from Burrell. (Courtesy of George Robinson.)

Norman Hall donned his US Navy uniform before going off to serve his country in World War II. Hall is standing in front of his parents' home on the west prong of Jackson Creek, just off Lovers Lane. (Courtesy of Norman Hall.)

Just a few months after World War II ended the community celebrated the sacrifice of those who fought in the war. The Deltaville Improvement Association unveiled a large plaque with names of all those in the community who fought in the war. Speeches and music were part of the ceremony held in front of the community center. (Courtesy of Garland Robins.)

After the Deltaville Improvement Association unveiled this plaque, "honoring these men who served in the Armed Forces of our country," it stood for many years as a reminder of the sacrifice Deltaville men and women made for their country. (Courtesy of Betsy Hudgins.)

Norton Hurd was a member of the flight team Hell Razors and flew in the first group of Navy planes to bomb Tokyo. After surviving a showdown with a Japanese fighter near Chi-Chi Jima, one of his engines failed, and he crashed into the Pacific. He survived and was awarded the Distinguished Flying Cross, given to those who distinguished themselves by heroism. (Courtesy of Norton Hurd.)

Deltaville men and women were involved in every American armed conflict, going back to the Revolutionary War. Theodore "Bug" Deagle (right) was one of many young men who took part in World War II and came home after the war to live their lives in the community. (Courtesy of Willard and Shirley Norris.)

Members of the 1964 Deltaville Little League baseball team are, from left to right, (first row) Wayne Walden, David Johnson, Jimmy Mears, Willard "Tuna" Norris Jr., Jack Hurd, and Roy "Boggie" Jackson; (second row) Al Hudgins, Benjy Callis, Edmond Harrow Jr., George Willard Jackson, and Gerald Wilson; and (third row) manager Willard Norris Sr., Terry Taylor, Al Selby, and manager Oran Johnson. (Courtesy of John M. Bareford Jr.)

The Deltaville Little League team finished first in the 1963 Middlesex Little League season. The countywide league was founded in 1958 with four teams—Deltaville, Syringa, Urbanna, and Church View. George O. Cunningham Jr. (left), president of the league, presents Oran Johnson with a plaque as star-player Al Selby and coach Willard Norris watch. (Courtesy of John M. Bareford Jr.)

The 1965 Deltaville semipro baseball team played in the Rappahannock Baseball League and went 13-3 in the win-loss column that year. Members are, from left to right, (first row) Jimmy Johnson, Rueben Lemons, Danny Whitaker, Philip Armstead, Gene Sutton, and Johnnie Fleet; (second row) Mickey Ward, Howard Hall, Bobby Faulkner, Jerry Ward, Donald Fitchett, coach Edwin Figg, and manager Fred Crittenden. (Courtesy of John M. Bareford Jr.)

Members of the 1940 Deltaville baseball team are, from left to right, (first row), Speck Harrow, Bobby Ailsworth, Raymond Perry, Edward Norton, Norton Hurd, and Mutt Carlton; (second row) Alfred Norris, Clabryn Bridger, Eugene Harrow, John Fleet, Eugene Ruark, and Edmond Harrow. Deltaville is a baseball town to this day; the Deltaville Deltas, a semipro baseball team, play on summer nights in the community-run Deltaville Ballpark. (Courtesy of Norton Hurd.)

Team baseball started locally in the 1920s, and one legend of the field in the 1940s was Norton Hurd (pictured). Opposing players said he could "run like a deer." In the 1920s, it was George Harrow who could catch a ball as well with his bare hands as he could with a glove; in the 1930s, Roosevelt Walden was most remembered for a knockout punch against an opposing team's player. (Courtesy of Norton Hurd.)

Willard Norris played for the semipro Deltaville baseball team in the 1940s. The team played on a sandlot field at Stingray Point for many years and then the community built the Deltaville Ballpark in the 1950s. It is today one of the few community-lighted ballparks around. (Courtesy of Willard and Shirley Norris.)

Deer hunting and running hounds is a cool-weather sport for Deltaville hunters. Fred Crittenden (right), holding a dog, helps show off a trophy deer bagged sometime in the early 1960s. The Deltaville area is diverse when it comes to hunting; there are waterfowl of all kinds, deer, squirrel, rabbit, quail, and dove for area hunters. (Courtesy of Garland Robins.)

An event that took place at Stingray Point Hotel was E.W. Harrow's wild-game dinner. At the sixth annual event, those attending are, from left to right, (first row) Willie Blake Harrow, Garland Robins, Eddie W. Harrow, W. Edward Norton Jr., and J. Oran Johnson; (second row) W. Edward Norton Sr., Edward P. Harrow, and Fred T. Crittenden. Venison, wild goose, wild duck, rabbit, and quail were all cooked by chef Victor Burrell. (Courtesy of John M. Bareford Jr.)

Deltaville hunt clubs provided sports and social activities for the men of the community. Pictured are members of a club showing off a prize deer of the day. Hunting and fishing have always played an important part in the lives of people in the community—for sustenance, sport, and as a way to provide fellowship to boost quality of life. (Courtesy of Garland Robins.)

Middlesex County Rescue Squad was the first organized rescue squad in Middlesex County. It began in the fall of 1958 in the garage of Claudia Marchant, where the first meetings were held. Pictured are, from left to right, squad members William Vaughan, Leonard Wright, Ryland Hall, and Addison Hall. The group had recently obtained a new boat to accommodate on-water emergencies. (Courtesy of the *Southside Sentinel*.)

The Middlesex County Rescue Squad and Lower Middlesex County Volunteer Fire Department shared a building in 1970, when this photograph of rescue squad members was taken. Those pictured are, from left to right, Addison Hall, Dr. Harold W. Felton, Gladys Prince, Aubrey Hudgins, Ryland Hall, Rev. David Brown, Goldie Croxton, Patsy Watson, Frank Medicus, Bobbie Taylor, and Dale Taylor. (Courtesy of the *Southside Sentinel*.)

The Deltaville Recreation Center, as the community center was called in 1971, was used as a voting site for the New Market Precinct. Pictured at right is New Market election clerk B.D. Wake handing a ballot to Wade Stewart as Garland Robins awaits his turn. New Market in the 1800s was a defined community, as an 1830s county deed states that "the main road leads from Sandy Bottom to New Market." (Courtesy of the *Southside Sentinel*.)

In 1964, one of the most active female organizations in the Deltaville Community was the Degree of Pocahontas of the Improved Order of Red Men. The group was a branch of the Cheyenne Tribe 120 Improved Order of Red Men. Although the Red Men organization no longer exists, the old lodge building is still standing near the community ballpark. (Courtesy John M. Bareford Jr.)

Donna Chapter No. 179 of the Order of the Eastern Star 964 officers in 1964 are, from left to right, (first row) Ann Ward, Irene Jackson, Dr. Harold Felton, Marie Felton, EvaLeigh Estes, John Estes Jr., and Wade Crittenden; (second row) Shirley Mears, Lucille Jackson, Dorothea Houston, Louise Miller, and Ailean Mercer; (third row) Martha Parker, Mary Wake, Alice Rose, Ida Bridger, and Alfred Bridger Jr.; (fourth row) Vivian Wilson and Grace Green. (Courtesy of John M. Bareford Jr.)

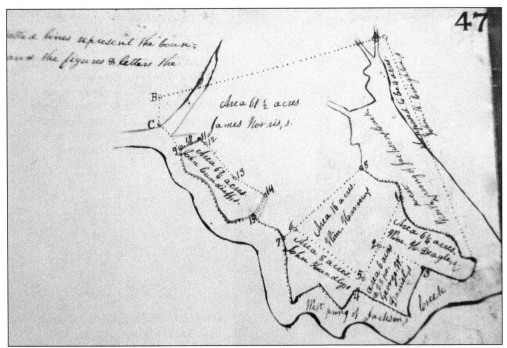

This 1820s survey shows the Lover's Lane area between the prongs of Jackson Creek. Several landowners' last names are still familiar. James Norris owned 61 acres; William Harrow, 16 acres; William Deagle, 6 acres; and George Daniel, 6 acres. (Courtesy of Middlesex County Clerk's Office.)

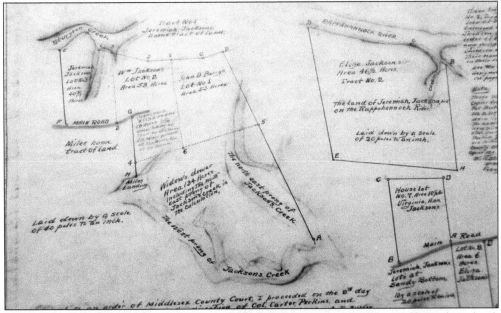

The Jackson family were large landowners when this 1820s survey was done of the southern bank of Sturgeon Creek; portions of Jackson Creek and lots on the main road were owned by Jeremiah, Eliza, Virginia, and Ann Jackson. Most likely, the name Jackson Creek is from that family name. The survey also shows that "Sandy Bottom" was being used then as the name of the community. (Courtesy of Middlesex County Clerk's Office.)

A tornado struck the village about dusk in September 1935. Molly Deagle's store that was located at the end of Lovers Lane near Jackson Creek Public Dock was blown off its foundation. Written on the back of one of the photographs is "crowd in store some got hurt." Lad and Lewis Wright were slightly injured during the blow, it states. (Courtesy of John M. Bareford Jr.)

The Harrow clan, children of Earl and Annie Harrow who lived on Lovers Lane on Jackson Creek, poses for this 1945 photograph. Pictured are, from left to right, Earline Adeline Harrow (Perkinson); Laura Frances Mae Burruss (Watts), an aunt; Bernard Raymond Harrow; Katherine Marie Harrow (Batley); and Eleanor Lavinia Harrow (Hudgins). (Courtesy of Diane [Batley] Dalsaso.)

This photograph of the Ruark family children was taken in 1906. Pictured are, from left to right (first row) Edwin Rufus Ruark, Julia Kennard, and Laura Katherine Ruark (Harrow); (second row) Lannie Filmore Ruark, Thomas Henry Ruark, and Willie Warner Ruark. The area in Deltaville known as Ruark is named from the Ruark family. (Courtesy of Charles A. Ruark.)

Shirley Harrow (left), Billy Wright (center), and Marie Batley sit on the deadrise charter boat *Miss Ruth*, owned by Capt. Edmond Harrow Sr., in Jackson Creek about 1938. The children were watching family members fish from the dock when this photograph was snapped. (Courtesy of Willard and Shirley Norris.)

Shirley Harrow and Willard Norris are pictured here just a few months away from their honeymoon. Shirley graduated from high school in June 1945 and they were married in August. They have lived in Deltaville their entire lives on the road called Lovers Lane. Pictured in the background are Willard's 1939 Plymouth Coupe and cottages at Stingray Point. (Courtesy of Shirley and Willard Norris.)

After World War II, Richmond families began to purchase summer homes in the area. The Strotmeyer family (above) from Richmond began coming to Ruark in the early 1930s to rent a cottage from the Ruark family each summer. In the 1940s, the family purchased Capt. Al Ruark's home. Often, mothers and children spent the entire summer in Deltaville while husbands and older sons came down on weekends. (Courtesy of Bob Strotmeyer.)

Dr. William R. Gwathmey married Ora Vaughan of Deltaville and was the doctor there from about 1900 until his death in 1933. A great hunter, Dr. Gwathmey always had a bird dog. At his death, his last dog, Billy, would not allow anyone to get near the casket that was in the living room. Daily, he fetched the paper for the doctor, so a nephew yelled to Billy to go get the paper for Uncle William, and the dog went out the door. (Courtesy of Caroline Jones.)

Robert Dea Ailsworth, known as Captain Dea, and Lelia Bratten Ailsworth are pictured here in 1916. They were parents of 11 children, and Captain Dea made his living running freight boats. He owned the *Lillian T.* and the *J.C. Drewer* and used these boats to buy oysters and to haul freight. (Courtesy of Alfred E. Ailsworth Jr.)

A young Willard Norris sports his 1936 Ford Coupe powered by a flathead V-8 engine. Norris bought the car used in 1942 and hardly looks old enough to have a driver's license. (Courtesy of Willard and Shirley Norris.)

North Inn Plantation was owned by John and Hilda McGuirk, who had a business making Christmas decorations for Miller & Rhodes and Thalhimers department stores in Richmond. The decorations were made in the basement of North Inn and local Deltaville folk worked in the business. Pictured are, from left to right, Nettie Williams, Mary Ruark, Maxine Blake, Tom Burke, and Lorraine Stewart. (Courtesy of the Deltaville Maritime Museum.)

Margaret Moffitt poses sitting on this car fender in 1939. Automobile fenders and running boards have been used to stage some wonderful photographs over the generations. When automobiles were relatively new to the world, they inspired some lovely photography. (Courtesy of Garland Robins.)

The 1964 Harvest Queen of the Improved Order of Red Men and the Degree of Pocahontas for District 5 Paulette Green of Deltaville (holding flowers) and her court rode in Deltaville's annual Independence Day parade. The name of the annual parade and festivities was later changed to Heritage Day. (Courtesy of John M. Bareford Jr.)

Deltaville has had its fair share of beauty queens, such as Alvine Taylor (left), who won the title Miss Rappahannock in a 1940s regional beauty contest. Taylor would eventually marry Deltaville's own World War II hero Norton Hurd, and they would make Deltaville their home. (Courtesy of Garland Robins.)

Susan Harrow (left) of Deltaville won the local Junior Miss title at the 1971 Urbanna Oyster Festival. In this photograph, she is on her way to the Virginia Junior Miss Pageant in Roanoke. (Courtesy of the *Southside Sentinel*.)

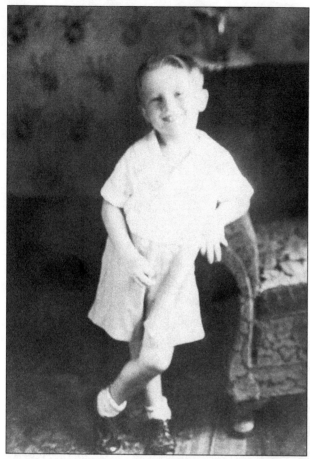

A little Willard Norris resembles Spanky from the *Our Gang* short films of the 1930s and early 1940s, which were shown on television under the title *The Little Rascals*. The Norris family has lived in Deltaville since the mid-1800s and its members made their livings working the water, charter boat fishing, and building boats. Willard has done all three. (Courtesy of Willard and Shirley Norris.)

Duck Ruark was three years old when he went out to play on this slab woodpile that his father Tom Henry Ruark had brought from Baltimore on the schooner *Maggie* to fire the family woodstove. (Courtesy of Charles A. Ruark.)

Capt. J. Dewey Norton was considered the dean of charter boat fishing in Virginia as the Deltaville native caught this 58-pound, 8-ounce striped bass in 1963 and held the state record for the largest striper for nearly 20 years. (Courtesy of Betsy Hudgins.)

Irving Taylor (left) of Taylor's Restaurant and Capt. Dewry Norton shows off the 58-pound, 8-ounce striper caught by Norton. A charter boat captain, Norton fished out of Jackson Creek. (Courtesy of Betsy Hudgins.)

This rare photograph shows Eugene Ruark, a man all about boats, riding a horse. Ruark owned and operated a marina on Fishing Bay and was a builder of deadrise and cross-plank sailing skipjack vessels. (Courtesy of Gene Ruark.)

Dr. Buzzy Council started coming to Deltaville with his parents in 1925 and retired from the medical profession only to move to the river and take up building models of Deltaville deadrise boats. (Courtesy of the *Southside Sentinel.*)

Early swimming pools in the area were built to accommodate visitors as the Horse Point Inn on the Piankatank River, and Healy Creek installed this pool in 1953 to encourage city folk to come down and enjoy Deltaville's outdoor atmosphere. (Courtesy of Billy and Mabel Williams.)

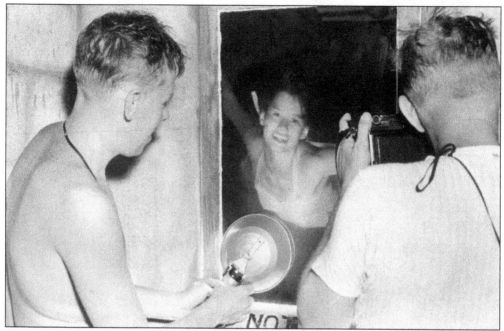

One of the features of the new swimming pool at Horse Point Inn was a window, which allowed underwater photographs to be taken of swimmers. The inn offered a recreational setting and amenities that attracted visitors from far and wide. When they came and found the inn, they often found Deltaville too, visiting again to fish and sail. (Courtesy of Billy and Mabel Williams.)

Yacht Club, Deltaville, Va.

Members of the Urbanna Yacht Club, founded in 1939, purchased land on Fishing Bay in 1949 to move their sailing club closer to Chesapeake Bay. A ground breaking was held on April 24, 1949, at a site that offered an ideal combination of a sheltered racecourse for small, one-design sailboats and a safe harbor for mooring of cruising yachts. (Courtesy of Jere and Paula Dennison.)

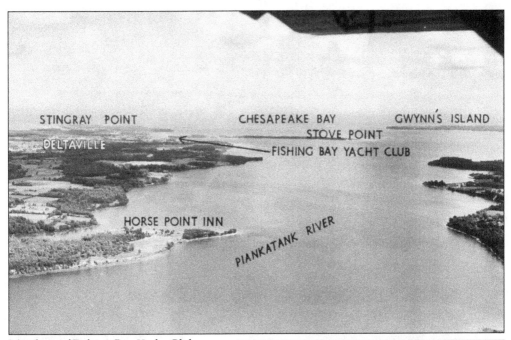

STINGRAY POINT   CHESAPEAKE BAY   GWYNN'S ISLAND
STOVE POINT
DELTAVILLE   FISHING BAY YACHT CLUB

HORSE POINT INN   PIANKATANK RIVER

Members of Fishing Bay Yacht Club can sail either out of Fishing Bay or Jackson Creek, as it is located on the banks of both bodies of water. (Courtesy of Billy and Mabel Williams.)

The aura, fun, and delight of sailing brings many people to the shores of Deltaville to cruise in small or large crafts. The marina business is one of the largest industries in the region. Fresh air, salt water, and steady Chesapeake Bay winds keep sailors coming back to the community. (Courtesy of Billy and Mabel Williams.)

Whether on Broad, Jackson, Sturgeon, Hunting, Moore, Coves, or Healy Creek, children find the water. What better way to swim than with a straw hat and a bonnet? Generations of Deltaville folks recall with fondness the times they spent down on the creek bank. (Courtesy of Garland Robins.)

The annual Deltaville Fourth of July celebration has been going on for many years in town. American flags are flown throughout the community, including on the fronts of automobiles. (Courtesy of the *Southside Sentinel.*)

Taylor's Marina was third in the float category at the 1970 Fourth of July Parade with its "Welcome to Deltaville, Come Fish and Relax" theme. (Courtesy of the *Southside Sentinel.*)

Wilson's Service Center sponsored the clowns in the 1971 Independence Day parade. The community of Deltaville has held celebrations on the Fourth of July for decades, going back to the 1940s when powerboat races on Fishing Bay were part of the festivities. (Courtesy of the *Southside Sentinel*.)

For years, the Middlesex County Lions Club has met at Taylor's Restaurant in Deltaville. The new officers in 1970 are, from left to right, Ralph Belknap, Games Dozier, C.D. Mattox, Carl Prince, Billy Bryant, Meredith Mckenney, Johnny Williams, and R.W. Fary. (Courtesy of the *Southside Sentinel*.)

Dr. William R. Gwathmey gives treats to his hunting dogs at his home at Ruark. The building behind him is his office, which still stands today. His patient is by the tree, waiting for his attention. George ?, who worked at the home, is holding Dr. Gwarthmey's horse, Ripple. (Courtesy of Caroline Gwathmey Jones.)

Woodport was home to William Conrad and family, who owned the property from 1868 to 1900. Conrad's Steamboat Landing, located on the waterfront near Woodport, was named for the Conrad family. Historically, Woodport is tied to Zoar Baptist Church, now located in the heart of Deltaville. An owner of Woodport, John R. Taylor donated land in 1836; an early church structure was built there near Chick Cove Farm. (Courtesy of Beverly and Jamie Barnhardt.)

The home of Alton Prince on Lovers Lane was demolished in the tornado of 1935 and his barn was turned up on its side. On the back of one photograph, it noted that Doris Prince and Mary Thomas were inside the home and injured in the storm. (Courtesy of John M. Bareford Jr.)

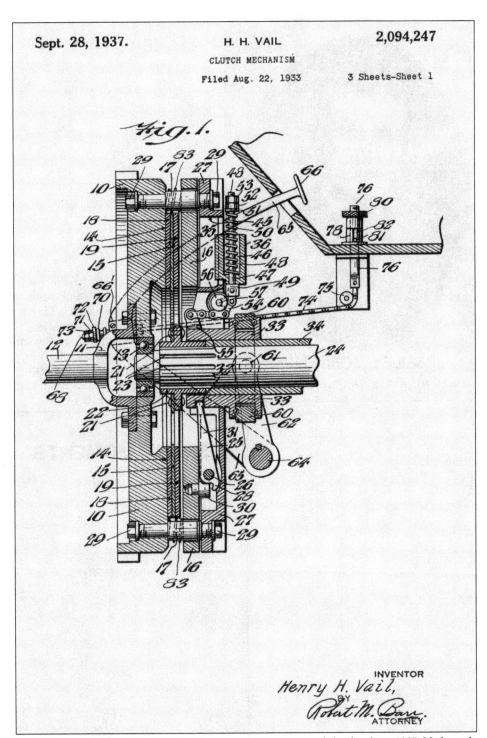

Fig. 1.

INVENTOR

Henry H. Vail,

BY

Robert M. Barr.

ATTORNEY

Deltaville inventor Harry Vail received a patent on an automobile clutch in 1937. Vail was born in 1876 and died in 1943. He and his wife, Lulie Games Vail, operated a chicken farm across the road from where the Deltaville Community Center is located today. He also taught building trades at Syringa High School. (Courtesy of Deborah Dozier Haynes.)

J. BAILEY CORNELIUS

BORN IN DELTAVILLE, VA., 22nd OF MARCH, 1862

The poet laureate of Deltaville was J. Bailey Cornelius, who built boats at his railway on Jackson Creek. He later moved to Baltimore and published *Spare Moments*, an anthology of poems that reflected his life. Cornelius's love of Deltaville and Jackson Creek is obvious in his poems. (Both, courtesy of Edna Deagle Shackelford.)

"SPARE MOMENTS"

A BOOK OF POEMS

-----------BY-----------

J. BAILEY CORNELIUS

1920

PRICE 60 CENTS

Barbara Jackson of Deltaville was head drum majorette for the marching band of Middlesex High School in 1965. Most of the squad was from the lower end of Middlesex County near Deltaville. Pictured above are, from left to right, Connie French, Mary Brooks, Barbara Jackson, Claudia Robins, and Paulette Topping. (Courtesy of John M. Bareford Jr.)

During the days of community schools, Wilton Elementary School served Deltaville and mothers worked hard in the local PTAs to make the school better. Pictured, from left to right, are newly elected PTA officers Lucina Crittenden, Frances Johnston, and Betty Harrow and installer Mabel Clark. (Courtesy of John M. Bareford Jr.)

Boatbuilder Bryan Miller (right) and owners of the *William Bowe* pose for a photograph at the launching on Fishing Bay. Miller and other descendants of boatbuilders carried on the tradition of building commercial fishing boats into the latter years of the 20th century. (Author's collection.)

The men of Deltaville often made their livings working the water. The Chesapeake Bay patent-tong clam fishery is all but gone today, but in the 1980s, the dean of bay clammers, Dink Miller, went to work most days. Dink was a "hard driver" and worked in the worst of weather. This photograph was taken in the 1980s on a rough day near the cut channel in Chesapeake Bay. (Author's collection.)

Hugh Norris was a schooner captain, boatbuilder, and waterman; towards the end of his years, he knitted crab-net bags for local crabbers. He used a gooseneck rocking chair handle to support the net as he wove the string back and forth. Behind him on the wall is a painting of the Stingray Point lighthouse, painted by his neighbor Lewis Wright, an artist and boatbuilder. (Author's collection.)

JACKSON CREEK, VA.

This 1933 photograph gives the impression that Deltaville is a very rural community, and at the time it was. However, the desire to own waterfront property and recreational boating interests changed all that as home building and commerce grew. Today, the waterfront is lined with houses and the community is thriving. (Courtesy of Middlesex County Museum.)

BIBLIOGRAPHY

"A Brief History of Zoar Baptist Church." *Southside Sentinel*, November 27, 1958.

Beta Sigma Phi Sorority. *A Portrait of Deltaville*. Richmond, VA: William Byrd Press, 1976.

Bogger, Tommy L., PhD. *A History of African Americans in Middlesex County, 1646–1992*. White Stone, VA: Nohill Inc., 1995.

Burgess, Robert H. *Chesapeake Circle*. Cambridge, MD: Cornell Maritime Press, 1965.

Burgess, Robert H. and Graham H. Wood. *Steamboats Out Of Baltimore*. Cambridge, MD: Tidewater Publishing, 1968.

Burgess, Robert H., and William A. Fox, eds. *Chesapeake Sailing Craft*. Centreville, MD: Tidewater Publishers, 2005.

Chamberlayne, C.G. *The Vestry Book of Christ Church Parish Middlesex County, Virginia, 1663–1767*. Richmond, VA: Old Dominion Press, 1927.

Chowning, Larry S. *Chesapeake Legacy Tools and Traditions*. Centreville, MD: Tidewater Publishers, 1994.

———. *Deadrise and Cross-planked*. Centreville, MD: Cornell Maritime Press, 2007.

———. "Stingray Point Lighthouse: Bay Scenes of Yesteryear Are Recalled." *Southside Sentinel: A Summer to Remember Supplement*, 1982.

Chowning, Larry S. and Archie Soucek, eds. *Signatures in Time—A Living History of Middlesex County, Virginia*. Saluda, VA: Middlesex County Board of Supervisors, 2012.

Gray, Louise E., Evelyn Q. Ryland, and Bettie J. Simmons. *Historic Buildings in Middlesex County Virginia 1650–1875*. Charlotte, NC: Delmar Printing, 1978.

Leyden, Don. *Philippi Christian Church (DOC) Deltaville, Virginia, Established 1871—A Brief History*. Deltaville, VA: Philippi Christian Church, 2010.

Norton, Randolph. "Deltaville Reminiscences—The Tabernacle." *Southside Sentinel*, December 8, 1988.

Visit us at
arcadiapublishing.com

Printed in the USA
CPSIA information can be obtained
at www.ICGtesting.com
LVHW051046290923
759703LV00005B/15